T0032069

Andrea Marcolongo is an Italian journalist, writer, scholar, and former speech writer for Prime Minister Matteo Renzi. Her books include *The Ingenious Language* (Europa, 2019) and *Starting from Scratch: The Life-Changing Lessons of Aeneas* (Europa, 2022). She lives in Paris, France.

Will Schutt is the author of *Westerly*. His translations for Europa Editions include *The Ingenious Language* and *Starting from Scratch* by Andrea Marcolongo, *The Breaking of a Wave* by Fabio Genovesi, and *Elena Ferrante's Key Words* by Tiziana de Rogatis.

THE ART OF RUNNING

ALSO BY

ANDREA MARCOLONGO

The Ingenious Language

Starting from Scratch:
The Life-Changing Lessons of Aeneas

Andrea Marcolongo

THE ART OF RUNNING

Learning to Run Like a Greek

*Translated from the Italian
by Will Schutt*

Europa
editions

Europa Editions
27 Union Square West, Suite 302
New York NY 10003
www.europaeditions.com
info@europaeditions.com

Copyright © 2022, Gius. Laterza & Figli, All rights reserved.
First Publication 2024 by Europa Editions

Translation by Will Schutt
Original title: *De arte gymnastica. Da Maratona ad Atene con le ali ai piedi*
Translation copyright © 2024 by Europa Editions

All rights reserved, including the right of reproduction
in whole or in part in any form.

*This work has been translated with support from
the Italian Ministry of Culture's Centro per il libro e la lettura.*

CENTRO
PER IL LIBRO
E LA LETTURA

Library of Congress Cataloging in Publication Data is available
ISBN 979-8-88966-033-0

Marcolongo, Andrea
The Art of Running

Cover design and illustration by Ginevra Rapisardi

Prepress by Grafica Punto Print—Rome

Printed in Canada

CONTENTS

To Luis Miguel, without a doubt

Socrates: I think the earliest inhabitants of Greece, like many foreigners today, took the sun, moon, earth, stars, and sky for gods. And because they saw that these things were always racing about, they called them gods (*theous*), for it was in their nature to run (*thein*). And afterward, when they recognized other divinities, they called them by the same name.

—PLATO, *Cratylus*

If you're standing still, walk.
If you're walking, run.
If you're running, fly.
—CICERO, *Letter to Atticus*, Volume II, 23

God rarely lets a man run the race of his life
from start to finish without stumbling or falling.
—PHILO OF ALEXANDRIA

If I dream at night, I dream I'm a marathoner.
—EUGENIO MONTALE

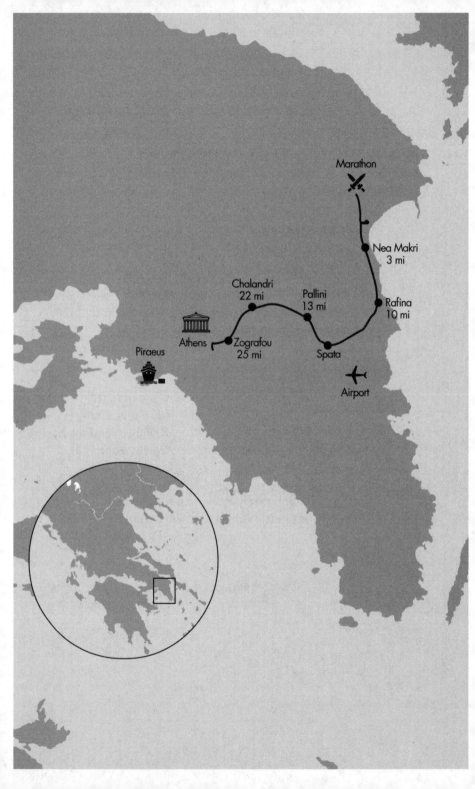

enikékamen. We have won.

Legend has it that was all the Greek messenger Philippides managed to say after running the first ever marathon in 490 BC. Then he dropped dead from exhaustion.

Before we accept the ill portents of those original, fateful twenty-five miles traveled at a trot, it's worth going over the matter for a minute. Because that might not be the whole truth.

For starters, Philippides may have been called Pheidippides, at least according to the historian Herodotus, who first told the story of the legendary hemerodrome. In ancient Greece, the name hemerodrome (literally day-runner, from *heméra*, or day, and *drómos*, from the root of *dramein*, to run) was given to messengers who could cover long distances on foot and deliver dispatches from one city to another.

Whatever his name was, Philippides must have been in amazing shape if, as Herodotus writes in *Histories*, he traveled 140 miles in two days to ask the Spartans to join Athens in its bloody war with the Persians. And that's not all. Apparently during his long trek the messenger had time to stop and listen to the god Pan complain that the Athenians didn't worship him.

The next version, which solidified Philippides' reputation as the first marathon runner in history, would have to wait for Plutarch, a writer at work in the first century AD, long after the events of the story.

In *On the Fame of the Athenians*, the historian describes how, right after the decisive Battle of Marathon that marked the defeat of the Persian King Darius, a soldier still in uniform ran all the way to Athens to spread word of the historic victory. But the poor man only had time to say, "We've won!"—nenikékamen is practically a proverb now—before he keeled over, killed by excessive fatigue.

Plutarch says he's unsure of the hero's name, but no such concerns troubled Pausanius and Lucian. For these two writers, it had to have been Philippides, the most famous hemerodrome in all Greece.

Scholars have tried for centuries to resolve inconsistencies in the legend of the original marathon, often casting doubt on its historical accuracy. Besides the uncertainty surrounding the spelling of his name, it appears unclear why a runner as fit as Philippides, capable of covering in two days the 140 or so miles separating Athens and Sparta, would have dropped dead after having run "just" over twenty-five.

Whatever happened, there is hardly a marathon runner today who hasn't nurtured hopes of one day matching the first Greek long-distance runner step for step upon hearing the legend. It's a sign that we all need a little poetry in our lives, especially when we're running.

One important clarification—I myself was confused for a long time—and a fun etymological fact:

When speaking of the distance between Athens and

Marathon, the *demos*, or village, that lends its name to the greatest of footraces, I wrote twenty-five miles. Today, anyone who has broken in a pair of sneakers knows that's not your standard marathon.

But it was not until the 1908 Summer Olympics in London that the coveted 26.2 miles was established, when the Prince of Wales made a whimsical request to start the race at the gardens of Windsor Castle so that the royals could watch from their comfortable perch in the shade. As a result, subsequent runners have been forced to schlep an extra four hundred yards before they can say, "We've won!"

As for the fun fact, the word marathon has nothing to do with running. The name of the city, today the site of a small, delightful museum dedicated to the sport, comes from the Greek word for fennel, an herb commonly found in the level field where the famous battle against the Persians was fought. Marathon literally means "place full of fennel."

There is no denying the fact that ancient myths are alluring.

But the (tragic, sure) beauty of Philippides' story mitigates none of the hard work needed to run a marathon.

My own modest (read: insignificant) tally of achievements precludes me from telling the story of epic triumphs and mythic finishes in this book. Having never run twenty-five miles straight, I could not care less that today's race is four hundred yards longer than the original. To my mind, every inch is a symbol and leviathan of titanic effort.

Yet the years I spent wrestling with the Greek language in order to think like the Greeks has made me change tactic. After all that time poring over textbooks and dictionaries at a desk, I now feel compelled to stand up and attempt to run like the Greeks.

Because one thing is certain. Everything has changed since Philippides' time: technology, politics, science, war; our way of writing, eating, traveling. We've even proven capable of ruining the climate! But two things have remained unchanged: our anatomical makeup (the muscles with which we're equipped are the exact same as the muscles that once coiled around the quick bones of the Greeks) and those damn twenty-five miles separating Marathon from the Acropolis.

I think, or I'd like to think, that two constants are much more than a sign—not a guarantee of anything, but excellent odds.

So, to make something out of that rude awakening that was my setting out to run after years bent over a Greek dictionary, I want to retrace the route that the courier Philippides took—strong of body and sound of mind. I just hope that my story doesn't come to the same tragic end.

INTRODUCTION

> As soon as children have learned to read and write and are able to understand the written word, they are made to read the works of the most important poets and learn them by heart . . . This is also the time when parents send their children to a physical education teacher [a trainer] to improve their bodies and teach them discipline, so that any physical shortcomings will not make them fear war or action.
>
> —PLATO, *Protagoras*

In my thirty-five years, only two things, aside from my mother, have delivered me into this world. Two things that haven't changed my life, so to speak, as much as led me to understand life and, in the end, live.

The first was ancient Greek, which I encountered in the classrooms at my *liceo classico* when I was fourteen. The second was running, which I encountered along the Seine at the end of summer three years ago.

It is about this second discovery—epiphany, really—that I intend to talk in this book. I've already said more than enough about the language of ancient Greece and don't see any point in adding anything further; if I bring it up now and again in this preface, it isn't to inflict pain on the reader but to help me better understand and think through things, for I hope the comparison will shed light on how I currently feel about running, which, for the sake of convenience, can be described in a word: confused.

Nothing. That was the extent of my knowledge of running, or racing, or jogging—call it what you will—when I put on a pair of running shoes for the first time. Absolutely zilch. And apart from a handful of totally unmemorable outings, the same could be said of all my firsthand experiences in that parallel universe we call sports. As for secondhand experience, the passive enjoyment taken, as a spectator, in the human spectacle of competitive sports, I could boast of a bit more expertise. But save for a curiosity in soccer as intermittent as it was willed and which compelled me to the stadium a couple times, it never amounted to more than that generic admiration and awe that comes over us all when we watch the human body in motion while parked on the couch or in the bleachers.

And here we arrive at the first, surprising point of similarity between my foray into running and the path that led me to one day pick up an ancient Greek dictionary: I had absolutely no prior knowledge of either subject. Worse, before stumbling upon them, I barely suspected that Greek or running even deserved a prominent place in my boring existence.

To be clear, not only were there no Greek enthusiasts in my humble family, but there also wasn't a single distant relative who had graduated from a *liceo classico*—nothing too Dickensian there, it's just the way it was. That's why a public school education is important. It is strange that it only now occurs to me that the dearth of humanists in my household was equal to the dearth of athletes. Aside from the obligatory bicycle given to me as a present when I was about eight, I don't remember ever having seen sports equipment being carried into our house. Nor did it cross my mind to demand any.

Somehow, I made the two discoveries independently and in my modestly pioneering way. In both cases, it fell to me to seek them out in what until then had been terra incognita.

The one, not insignificant difference is that, when I got it into my head to learn the Greek alphabet, I had at my back the innocent and brash wind of a newly minted teenager. Whereas when I put on a pair of running shoes for the first time, that wind was about to die down for good.

The outcome of these two discoveries, in any case, is identical: despite my ardor and determination, I remain an amateur in both fields. At the age of thirty-four, I have neither a doctorate in classical philology to hang on the wall nor medals to show off the finish lines my legs have carried me across. For years I publicly proclaimed my love and dedication until I was out of breath, yet in both arenas, Greek and running, I am still way behind the professional and competitive curve.

So, just as my first book was not meant to be taken for an ancient Greek textbook, this one should not be considered definitive, scientific, or exhaustive. It is no more than the work of an amateur fortunate enough to have strong calves—and not much else. And therefore I don't claim to offer advice about running. If anything, I'd be grateful to get some! Nor am I here to promote methods for training. After all, they didn't yield great results when tested by this clueless author.

In all honesty, and with all the severity-verging-on-cruelty with which I tend to evaluate my achievements, I know that my propensity for amateurism can't be ascribed to weakness or laziness—not to them alone, anyways. I think it's more a consequence of the profession that I've chosen in life, which is to say writing. Whenever something really captures my interest, I almost never see it through to the end, out of some perverse need to leave it unfinished, so that I chastise myself for my shaky grasp of it yet at the same time take pleasure in writing about it.

I don't lack skills in ancient Greek or strength in my calves. And I don't believe, as Plato writes about sports, that I have ever shrunk from a war or battle, at least not the personal kind. But I must admit that I would never have written a book about Greek grammar had I had the courage to become a professor. And I would never have written about running had I already completed a marathon.

That must be the reason I run and write: to remain incomplete. Another form of cowardice.

I
On the Art of Gymnastics

Σ οφία. Science.
That is the very first word in the only ancient work on "gymnastics"—applied broadly, what today we call sports—to come down to us.

Not a pastime, then. Not a lesser alternative to the exercise of thought. Not fun and games. Neither a purely aesthetic act nor an obligation to stay in shape. Science, rigorous discipline—that is what ancient Greek philosophy meant by physical activity. A ξυγγενενεστάτην (natural) science for mankind, no less, because it appeared the moment humans came into the world.

The author of this brief, very intriguing study known in Latin as *De arte gymnastica* (On the Art of Gymnastics) was Flavius Philostratus, aka the Athenian, a teacher and philosopher born on the island of Lemnos around 170 AD, a time when Greek history had already become part of Roman history. A member of the Roman literary circle that assembled around Julia Domna, the enlightened wife of Septimius Severus, thanks to his fame Philostratus won a seat in the Senate before his death sometime between 244 and 249 AD.

Seven centuries, then, separate Philostratus from Pericles and Plato. To give you a sense of the enduring impact of that prodigious historical period that was classical Greece in the fifth century BC, that's the exact same number of centuries that separate us from Dante! With all its magnificent achievements, the period overshadows everything that came after in Greece. And because what swept through Greece following Phydias, Aeschylus, Pindar, and others was a blizzard of mediocrity, especially political mediocrity, later writers tried to identify the cause of this decline, one that relegated them to walk-on parts in literary history instead of elevating them to the heights of its founding fathers.

In *On the Art of Gymnastics* Philostratus is confident that the beginning of the end can be traced to the physical weakness of his contemporaries, a weakness he felt perfectly matched their trivial, flaccid modes of thinking. By then the triumphs of Greek athletes at the Olympics were a distant memory to be contemplated in the chipped marble statues of its winners and in the forgotten poems that sang of their exploits. In fact, as the philosopher writes, if "nature still [produced] lions no weaker than their ancestors, and the muscles of dogs, horses, and bulls [had] not gone slack; if trees, vines, and orchards [remained] as fertile as they once were and the hardness of gold, silver, and stones [hadn't] softened," then it stood to reason that the spiritual diminishment of men—who were, biologically speaking, unchanged—was due to laziness and lack of exercise.

But Philostratus wasn't just some pessimist. He was, above all, a great thinker. His primary goal was to show that playing sports isn't a mere hobby to get physical exercise but a requirement for buttressing one's mind.

As he writes at the start of his book:

> Let us consider the following pursuits as arts: philosophy, public speaking, poetry, music, geometry and, by Zeus, even

astronomy, so long as it is not carried to excess. Then there are the arts of organizing an army, of medicine, painting, and modeling [. . .] As for gymnastics, we believe that it is an art in no way inferior to all the others.

Of course I barely knew the name Philostratus before throwing myself into this all-encompassing project that running has become for me, and I had never read his invaluable and modern work on sports.

Both at high school and university, I (justifiably) spent entire weeks and months trying to crack the philosophies of the great authors of the classical world, arriving at such abstract lines of reasoning that, especially at that age, the ancient Greeks always seemed to me obscenely intelligent giants who took little interest in squeezing and prodding their bodies. I had no problem picturing Plato in the act of honing his massive intellect, but I could never imagine him sweating on a sports field.

Aware as I was of the foundation of the first Olympics in 776 BC, at the time of Homer, and of Juvenal's *mens sana in corpore sano* (a sound mind in a sound body), I understood the ancients possessed strong bodies and an enthusiasm for competitive sports. Yet I hadn't imagined that the Greeks, who in a handful of centuries set about mapping every single aspect of reality, from the physical circumference of Earth to the metaphysical circumference of the soul, had gone to the trouble of unpacking the meaning of sports.

Probably because I never played sports.

So, when I got my hands on Philostratus, I was expecting sensational revelations and—to my embarrassment now—had hoped to uncover god knows what kind of exercise plan in the age of Socrates that would have transformed me into a Homeric athlete.

That was ignorance, the result not only of my incompetence as a philologist and unfamiliarity with running shoes, but also of my maniacal approach to sports typical of our careless age.

An unlikely contributing factor was the recent pandemic, which revealed and exacerbated the trouble with our increasingly sedentary society, a society on the brink of immobility, where we are besieged from all sides—from national newspapers to social media to advertising to (more or less) organic food packaging, even to videogames—by people who want to teach us how to get fit, by workout routines that are proposed or publicized to us in the most random circumstances—many of which are, frankly, absurd. Staying in shape, then, has become an aesthetic and moral imperative, and that imperative has given rise to an industry that presumes to teach people the one thing they naturally know how to do as soon as they come into this world: to move, as Philostratus would put it.

Besides which exercises to do, we are increasingly reminded why we should exercise by a government that has been reduced to the role of kindly paterfamilias. Along with the recommendation to eat five portions of fruit and vegetables every day comes the friendly advice, from every corner of the market, from potato chip packaging to champagne labels, that we should exercise regularly to live a healthy life.

Michel Houellebecq might say that this utopian demand to live healthier and longer comes at the cost of joie de vivre. And this obsession with putting death off or being as thin as possible didn't actually interest the Greeks.

Philostratus wrote the first sports manual in history not because he wanted to convey the perfect Greek hero's workout routine or declare war on toxins. He wasn't trying to tell us how to play sports, or in what sequence to exercise our mortal muscles, or why we should exercise, compiling a list of practical benefits. At its core his book seeks to understand what sports are—and therefore what we talk about when we talk about physical activity.

Once I began to see that there was much more to running than a red face and aches and pains, understanding what we really mean by sports became more important to me than ever. In fact I quickly realized that the wellbeing I felt after exercising—and, on the rare occasion, *while* exercising, whenever I plucked up the courage to put distance between myself and bed—wasn't limited to my muscles and their mechanical movement. My entire physical, mental, emotional, and spiritual being was set in motion, and it urged me to move so that I could gain a sense of wellness that went far beyond mere physical health.

To shed light on all this I leaned heavily on the theories of Philostratus' *On the Art of Gymnastics* while writing this book. For running, on the other hand, I relied on my own two legs.

I have to train for a marathon and I don't know where to start.

Let's begin with vocab, then.

I love the Italian verb used to convey how much one needs to train before a race. You don't take a stab or a shot at a race, in Italy you prepare for a race. As if you were preparing a cake, or preparing for an exam or date.

That is also the main reason I decided to write this book: to try to understand how, in an age that puts a premium on the slapdash and speedy, every year hundreds of thousands of people around the world willingly undertake the herculean efforts, the hard work and dedication that training for a race requires.

I now have five months to prepare to run those hallowed twenty-five miles between Marathon and Athens, a distance the mere sight of which, written down, fills me with apprehension (and fear). Five months isn't a lot of time but it's enough.

For a while I've been averaging four or five miles on my morning runs, a little more on the weekend. But, as on this windy May morning on the Seine, I don't run for any specific purpose; I run out of habit, motivated by a desire to feel well enough so that I can soon spend the rest of my day attending *to other things. Besides, there are runners who are satisfied to hit the road every day for decades and never even sign up for a marathon. No one is obligated to put themselves through the same agony as* Philippides. *I have run twelve miles straight once, and I have to admit it was really a rather nice experience, and it enabled me to take my running career a bit more seriously. Now I just need to run twice that far, I tell myself with forced optimism before my anxiety about Athens catches up with me.*

Though I may never have run a marathon, I can claim to have read everything now in circulation about how to train for one. For at least a year, I've been plundering newsstands, websites, and friends' experiences on my hunt for the best way to arrive prepared at the starting line and alive at the finish.

I don't know whether it's because I'm a nerd or a fretter— both, I think—but at a certain point my desk began filling up with running magazines and books that broadly speak about the subject. I followed blogs and Facebook pages. I studied the workout plans of every major fitness app. My research gave me intimate knowledge of the craziest marathoners in the world (runners unashamed to run naked and runners who run with their dogs, runners who run drunk and runners who go up and down the steps of Montmarte all night), of nearly every type of running shoe available, of the complete catalog of energy gels and bars, and, obviously, of the perfect diet for running. Yet I still hadn't found what I was looking for, something that would tell me what all this suffering and sacrifice was about.

The charts I downloaded and studied, with their weekly mile counts and workouts spread out over four months, are all alike. All of them tell you precisely how much your muscles and tendons will suffer when training for a marathon. But there's not a trace of poetry. No one tells you what you should be reading, who you should be thinking of, what music to listen to during each of these mammoth training sessions. More importantly, no one tells you why you should train. Sadly, there is no talk of beauty.

So I decided to follow a fairly common, roughly eighteen-week-long program and in the meantime seek answers from that which has always been, for me, a compass for navigating every hardship of existence: literature.

But this time my discoveries were rather thin. I soon realized that there are very few books that talk about running or in which the main character moves her legs when she's not in a hurry. And of these almost all are written by men.

Philostratus aside, no mention of running is made in ancient texts or later works. In canto three of the Inferno, Dante envisions running as a sadistic punishment for pusillanimous souls. Aside from technical essays and biographies of great athletes, I found only two books about running to set next to my running magazines: the French writer Jean Echenoz's Running, a fictionalized biography of the great Czech runner Emil Zátopek, and, not surprisingly, Haruki Murakami's What I Talk About When I Talk About Running.

Identifying with one of the greatest runners in recent history turned out to be impossible for me, but Murakami proved more pliable. I had already relished his book before I began to run, and rereading it after my initiation was both a comfort and a spur. However, a not insignificant detail separates me from the experience of the Japanese writer who for decades ran a marathon a year before moving on to triathlons and ultramarathons. I have yet to run a marathon and don't *even know if I'll pull it off! Nor for that matter am I a contender for the Nobel prize.*

In the end I had a flash of insight: I may never have run twenty-six miles, but I have written a book before. And not just one. That's a kind of endurance test, an intellectual marathon that always leaves me shattered, drained, feeling as though I've given it my all and then some and positive that I never want to hear talk of my subject again.

To prepare myself, then, all I have to do is apply to running the same curious (read: obsessive) gaze that I apply to the subjects I love and about which I intend to write. Whether it's Greek, the Aeneid, *or running, once I've decided that a subject is worth spilling ink over, I feel a sense of urgency so great, an almost physical need to understand, that I'd do anything to get to the bottom of it. If not kill someone, at least spend months and years dedicating every thought, every reading, every conversation to achieve my goal, tormenting my neurons and those of the person next to me.*

So that's how I intend to prepare for this marathon—and write this book. If it's impossible for me to think abstractly about racing without first experiencing a race, then it's equally hard for me to give my legs a workout unthinkingly. Every training session in view of Athens will be a chance for reflection, a way to exercise and test my ideas. Should I fail at one, then I'll fail at the other.

Ultimately this involves my once again writing a book, only this time instead of keeping my legs trapped underneath a desk I'll be writing while running. Maybe it won't work, but at least this way of preparing for a marathon motivates me and, in both cases, writing and running, cheers me up a little.

II
WHY WE RUN

Why I run I really don't know.

As I set about writing this book and planning every detail of my daily workout, which I hope will lead me to my first marathon in November, to my surprise I realized that I couldn't say why for the past three years I have insisted on lacing up my sneakers.

Sure, I could list a series of reasons, all high-minded, all equally cliched: peace of mind, the importance of staying in shape and leading a healthy lifestyle, the desire to stretch what I believe to be my limits and demonstrate to myself and others that my calves can hold me up for over twenty-five miles, etc. But that's not it. Not the whole of it, anyways.

Underneath these reasons, which seem torn from a self-help manual, lies the truth: I don't know why I run. And I don't know what irrational motive makes me swear, almost every time I run along the Seine, that it will be the last time, when it never is.

I have never been drawn to go on wild adventures for the sake of telling a story. I highly doubt that a few years from now I'll be at a dinner party gloating about the time I ran a marathon because, hey, it's a marathon. That the undertaking is considered mythic doesn't interest me all that much, certainly no more than the Paris-Dakar Rally (which I have *no* interest in) or swimming the English Channel.

The seductiveness of its being a 2,500-year-old race from Marathon to Athens has absolutely no bearing on the rock solid motivation that has me exercising constantly.

Indeed, I don't really care that the marathon is in Athens and not Chicago, at least as far as my performance is concerned. Not once has imagining myself running along the same path poor Philippides ran two thousand years ago brought me a shred of relief.

So there must be something else, besides the landscape in Attica or the finish line at the Panathenaic Stadium, where ancient athletes were once crowned with olive wreaths, that is setting my legs in motion and compelling me not to quit. Something deeper, which I'm not sure I can recognize—or maybe I don't want to discover.

Then one day, thinking more deeply about my apparent lack of motivation, I realized that my efforts are related to my terror of aging.

I finally understood, I think, that I keep running because it is the most concrete and effective way for me to feel alive, or at least the one way I know. In other words, I run because I'm afraid of dying.

* * *

"For those preparing for a major undertaking, I think it is very helpful not to deny them a crumb of faith," writes Philostratus in a short chapter about what appears to have always been the one thing people need in order to run: motivation. And perhaps somebody nearby who believes in them.

Not strength, not stamina, not a good stride or pair of sturdy knees. Since the very first book about running, writers have made it clear: all you need to make it through a run or a simple workout—Sunday jog included—is a good reason. A reason so sound that it makes up for the hard work, the frustration, the way your calves beg you just to quit, as well as that subtle but keen sense of ridiculousness that always, somewhere within the non-competitive runner, forces her to wonder, at least once a session, "Who's making me do this?"

A goal so indelible that it won't wash away with the first bead of sweat that drips down your forehead or with the thousands of more comfortable alternatives that the menu of life offers in lieu of running, that chore which, for common mortals, gets filed under the morning to-do list, not even time to get out of bed, or the evening, a little before slipping into it; and between them, a grueling day of work and family.

In short, to run, and continue running, one needs a reason tougher than any tendon, an unshakeable will to give it your all, without reservation or limits, to the bitter end— the same kind of will that led the first marathon runner in history to run to his death and beyond.

It must be acknowledged that, however shocking they may seem to us, the motivating forces of the ancients were far more convincing and persuasive than the notifications from apps that every runner uses (to each her own, depending on her taste) or texts from friends (should she choose to share the burden of her marathon training routine) or threats from one of the many different yet equally alienating smartwatches (which, once 6pm strikes, sound the alarm that she hasn't completed her 10,000 steps for the day).

When it came to establishing the best incentive for not giving up during a race, the Greeks were blunt, terse, and cutthroat, too. For them, it was life or death.

Even before the Greeks, the Egyptians had a law according to which any racer who came in second place after having been proclaimed winner of the previous race was to be put to death.

Athletes in Egypt literally risked their lives. It may be the only case in history where you'd be happy, and breathe a sigh of relief, to always finish last. An athlete could, however, have another person offer up their life in exchange for his own, maybe to take some of the pressure off during the race, though such volunteers were, evidently, scarce. That was not the case for Attalus the Egyptian, however. After he had been crowned victor, for his next race his coach offered up his life as collateral for Attalus's own. This gesture of unconditional loyalty, even at the risk of death, inspired the runner to achieve a second, even more resounding victory.

But athletic motivation was so deeply ingrained in the ancients that one time, in Greece, the Olympics were won by a dead man.

During a final round of pankration—a word that literally means "all of might," from *pan* (all) and *kratos* (might), a sport that combined boxing and wrestling and was strictly performed in the dust during the hottest time of day— Arrichion, already a two-time winner, felt the life going out of him. His coach then inspired in him a "love of death," as Philostratus writes—*erota tanatu*—saying, "Not giving up at the Olympics makes a fine shroud!"

According to sources, Arrichion died by strangulation while obstructing his opponent's feet and forcing him to call the fight. Whatever really happened, we know that the victory laurels were placed on the dead man's head. A statue of him was erected in the market of Phigalia, his hometown, to remind future generations of his feat.

Philostratus tells two other classic stories in which an athlete's motivation to continue to give it their all drew not on the dominion of death but on that of life, or love (the two are ultimately the same thing).

He writes that the fatherless Mandrogenes of Magnesia never once lost the will to run when his coach wrote the following words in a letter to his mother: "If they say your son is dead, believe it. But if they say he was defeated, never believe it."

More romantic is the story of Promachus of Pellene, a fighter crowned victor three times in the Isthmian Games, twice at the Nemean Games, and once at the Olympics. Promachus was known for having mean fists—he seems to have killed many of his opponents during boxing matches— and a tender heart. One day his coach realized that he had fallen in love, because during his workouts he did nothing but sigh and blush. His coach decided to resolve the situation by telling Promachus that the woman he loved would gladly go on a date with him if and only if he won the Olympics, which he proceeded to do, not only coming in first but defeating an opponent who among other things had a reputation for restraining lions with his bare hands.

For years I asked every runner I know, from the most diehard to the least disciplined, *why* they run, but none was able to give me a clear answer. They all offered a generic response: "well-being," of course, physical or mental. But one's reason for running can't be defined by that fleeting fistful of endorphins, since there are many human activities besides running that lead our brain to secrete these mood-enhancing neurotransmitters of gratification. You don't have to run like a madman to feel a little happy.

Ever since I decided to write this book, or live it, rather, for part of the practice of writing is inextricably linked to my training for a marathon, I do nothing but observe every runner that I encounter along the Seine and wonder: what's egging us on? What deep motivation is propping us up, guiding us, somehow compelling us to run? It's as if at a certain point this urge had turned us into slaves, and now look at us, cruising down bike paths and sidewalks at ten o'clock at night when other people are comfortably seated at a restaurant, or at six in the morning when the city is still asleep.

Then one January day I made a breakthrough in my efforts to figure out why for more than two thousand years human beings have been beset by running fever.

I was at the beach, in one of those unyielding, poetic winters that the tides of Brittany dole out. The coast was empty, the winter sea desolate as ever. The only ones there were me, my partner, and an older woman with two children (her grandchildren, I assumed) and a dog. When one of the two blond boys, busily collecting seashells, heard his grandmother calling him, he looked up, smiled, and started to run toward her, his little loyal dog nipping at his heels.

Then it hit me. When we're happy, we run *naturally*, with no pretense of exercising.

That's what kids have always done, it's impossible to make them sit still once they've been set free to play, to inhabit the cheerful season of childhood. And as adults, whenever we spot the person we love in a crowd, whether we're meeting them at an airport or on a date, we naturally break into a run, unembarrassed by how clumsy we look, reminded of the miracle of existence. We literally run to them.

Then there's the urge to take flight, the opposite of

running toward another person and more natural still. We run to reach someone; we run faster to get away from them.

That must have been the first reason human beings ran, day one of the evolutionary atomic bomb that let us inhabit this planet. Maybe that's the sole purpose of our legs: to flee from the first sign of trouble; clearly our brains are wired to sense danger and tell our muscles to run for it, since despite all our accomplishments and progress, they remain identical, in terms of primary fears and needs, to those of the first quivering Homo sapiens.

It's for this same reason that the most famous runner in movie history—innocent, heartbreaking Forrest Gump—begins the sprint that will one day lead him to crisscross the United States. His friend Jenny exhorts him to flee a group of bullies with a now legendary phrase: "Run, Forrest, run!"

In short, not counting sports, human beings *naturally* run for two related reasons: either because they're happy or because they're afraid. To meet someone or escape someone. Everything else, every other form of competitive determination, is no more than an attempt to make peace with one of those two impulses: happiness and fear. Or both.

To run after, to run from. That seems to me the crux of what drives millions of men and women to go out every day and run when they have no apparent need to.

Natural predators haven't roamed our streets for a long time (that is, if the laws of nature ever saddled human beings with a predator; the debate is ongoing). And yet the initial impression of flight and the later impression of conquest which every runner feels after a run have remained unaltered for thousands of years, and the ostensible restfulness after having ground out a few miles is still his or her immutable trophy.

I remember hearing a phrase on one of the many pod-casts about running that I listen to as relief from the bore-dom of my repetitive workouts. It went something like this: "There's no such thing as a runner who comes home after a run and feels worse than when he left."

That's it! That's exactly the point every runner in the world must admit to herself with disturbing clarity. We more or less consciously go for a run to escape our daily dose of stress, fatigue, frustration, expectations, and pres-sures. And, after a run, no matter how long or short, no matter how intense or leisurely, when we get home and slip into the shower we are, if not better, at least freer versions of ourselves.

Versions that, though not completely unburdened, are still a bit more compassionate. And, given our age-old struggle to balance happiness and fear, that may not be ev-erything, but it's a lot.

I never felt that chilling, quintessentially Greek "love of dying" that Philostratus counts among the incentives to run. But I do feel its exact opposite, every single God-given day. The terror of dying. An unbridled, foolish love of life.

To prove to myself that I'm alive, not just biologically but fully alive—emotionally, physically, spiritually—I know various activities, most of them quite pleasurable: being in love, going to an art exhibit, reading a good book, white wine on a balcony in the summer, the cool smell of fresh snow.

Yet, however sublime, these interests don't set my heart racing, as they say. They make me happy, but they don't actu-ally increase my heart rate much. Even when I feel genuinely well when in good company or facing a pretty view, my EKG doesn't register a significant change in the number of heart-beats required, in a state of rest, to get the blood pumping.

I'm generally not a fan of short-lived, heart-pounding, adrenaline-boosting thrills, whether it's extreme sports or drugs or horror movies. They're not my thing. So, by default, and maybe due to cowardice, the one activity that I know of and routinely perform to get my heartrate over its normal, aka life-as-usual, resting rate, is running.

When I run, I'm not getting on with my life; I'm living. I feel it with a precision and concreteness totally unknown to me prior to running, which even the most sublime mental activities fail to generate.

The life instinct that I feel when I run isn't cerebral, or confined to my head, or intimately poetic. It's not the (often bitter) fruit of my thoughts. When I run, I'm alive, physically and biologically, doing what I was programmed to do: pushing my body to its maximum physical potential. It's objective and observable, and it can easily be measured by the tools of science.

The blood pulsing in my veins and temples, my heart—suddenly audible, noisy even—magically falling into sync with my feet as they hit the pavement, my muscles warming up, reluctantly at first, then gladly: all do the job they are made to do. Running, my body performs every miraculous function for which it exists—nothing more.

That's life: tangible, mine. Indeed, I'm its spitting image, *life itself*, the celebration of every function written in my genetic code.

Every time I go for a run, long or short, my body and, by some miracle, my head along with it—that's what runners mean when they talk about "mental health"—does everything in its power to reach its one goal: to live life to the fullest, or at least far more than my body is permitted to when it's planted in a chair. My heart beats as fast as it can; my muscles contract as much as they can; my vascular system pumps as hard as it can; my brain, free of abstract thoughts, coordinates everything; my lungs swap carbon dioxide for oxygen. My whole body fulfills the duty that the DNA in every single cell demands. This completeness of motion, *pace* Philostratus, is a love of life. Nothing more, nothing less—and therefore everything.

It's because of this biological and emotional sense of wholeness that when you run you feel alive for once, complete for once. Sometimes even immortal.

Running is in fact the best antidote to my fear of dying. It's tangible proof, confirmation that, for today, and at least until tomorrow, I'm still in good health, still alive.

* * *

I think this vital impulse that every runner experiences while running has a lot to do with its opposite: the fear of aging, and therefore the fear of one day dying.

It's no coincidence that running is the first sign that the weather's changing and we're getting on in age. Most runners will readily admit that they didn't begin to run seriously, with consistency, discipline, ad hoc sportswear, workout routines and concrete goals, until they'd crossed the threshold of thirty.

In his magnificent memoir, Murakami recognizes this all too well when he writes about starting to run at the age of 33, the age "that Jesus Christ died. The age that Scott Fitzgerald started to go downhill." And though I entered the world of running in the middle of the journey of our life, with the aggravating factor that, like Dante, I found myself lost in a dark, if far earthlier, wood, I only recently discovered that marathons bear the burden of being seen as competitions for "old people."

It's true that professional long-distance runners are often over thirty years old, an age inconceivable for many other competitive sports, where, once you've reached twenty-five, you're already considered a has-been. It's true that, for reasons connected to the proper development of your cardiovascular and motor system—we're back to the full expression of the body I mentioned a moment ago—official footraces are essentially off limits to people under eighteen, an age when, in other sports, a final verdict has already been made as to the presence or absence of talent. It's equally true that, as I write this book, the world record for the marathon is held by the legendary Kenyan Eliud Kipchoge, born in 1984, which he set in 2018 in Berlin at two hours, one minute and thirty-nine seconds, and broke at an unofficial race in Vienna in 2019, coming in under two hours, a time long believed to be humanly impossible—especially for this author, who, though younger than Kipchoge, just hopes to return home in one piece after twenty-six miles, no matter how many hours, or even weeks, it takes.

Just look around you, on the streets and sidewalks, around the parks of our cities, at the starting line of every non-competitive race, every city run and trail race that now flood our calendars and have supplanted saints' days. Twenty-somethings are rare. All the runners are past thirty. Many of them way past.

Indeed, were you to suggest to a kid or teenager to go out "for a run," they'd be puzzled and say no. Not because they reject running a priori, but, for the young and very young, running is *part* of having fun. It isn't fun tout court.

Horsing around, playing make-believe, practicing other sports, children already run without the burden of training. Running, rather than resting, comes naturally to them, for "hopping about is essential to their age," as Philostratus writes in his treatise.

Moreover, all children seem naturally inclined to run away, as if they were escaping their parents' grasp, physically and metaphorically. In infancy the act of walking is seen as an imposition. They instinctively want to run, to come of age, while we adults keep saying, "There's no rush to grow up!" mistakenly convinced that we're keeping our children out of danger.

No child would ask a friend to go three laps around the field just to stay in shape or limber up. Children are already in the field chasing after a ball, building with blocks, flying kites. Running is just the starting point, the foundation of many other unforgettable childhood games, from hide-and-seek to capture-the-flag to cops and robbers.

When children eventually grow tired of "hopping about" and, for better or worse, new activities and occupations (school, friends, work) take its place, that remarkable, totally undemocratic wind that blows through when we're twenty makes up for our new condition of physical immobility. As is only right, in our twenties our bodies demand nothing more than that we live. A "love of life" flows through our veins night and day, like lava. We need no encouragement or long runs. With some cruel and unlucky exceptions, we don't have to take care of our bodies. We can abuse them all we want at night and the next morning wake up to find them in perfect shape. The head is overpoweringly determined to suck out all the marrow of life—the brain thirsts and hungers for life. We play sports to enjoy the company of others and have new experiences, certainly not to suffer. The kind of endurance that running puts to the test is of little (read: no) interest, because there is nothing to endure when we're busy learning how to live.

It's only afterward, when the wind we thought would blow forever begins to die down and without warning disappears for good, that we suddenly find ourselves interested in running, that activity which just the other day we hadn't given a thought to. On the contrary, we may have looked down on it as we watched that rainbow of older humanity intent on tiring itself out with long stretches of running.

I don't think it's looks alone, the desire to shrink our beer bellies or carve calves of steel, that is motivating the hitherto unthinkable urge to shop for running clothes or sign up for running blogs. In the long term, the looks factor turns out to be too weak an incentive to sustain the effort and determination that running demands. And even if our physiques might begin to change after just a few outings, our willpower flags.

I think it has more to do with that wind I mentioned, and the confirmation—at first so blurry and indistinct that you don't even have the courage to admit it aloud, then so obvious that denying it would be ridiculous—that the privileges of youth have come to an end. Forever.

Our peers also start gaining weight, sagging, getting wrinkles. Some even pass away. Suddenly that pitiless phrase "you're not twenty anymore" becomes more frequent. It's the burden of aging; death is no longer a distant prospect but part of the natural order of things.

"How beautiful is youth, which slips away from us!"

writes Lorenzo the Magnificent, before exhorting us to make the most of every moment. Slipping away again, starting over. And running.

Youth is the least democratic condition, and one day all of us will find ourselves evicted from it, kicked to the curb of adulthood, that tiring age of workouts and compromises.

So, rather than give in to despair out on that curb, we might as well pull on our sneakers. And make do. That's how more or less all runners get their start.

* * *

Along with motivation come—or should come, in an ideal world—motivators.

In his treatise, Philostratus writes about coaches ready to sacrifice their lives to prove that their faith in their athletes is unwavering and well-placed, as if they were lovers nervously awaiting the champion at the finish line or mothers with chests that swell with pride. And that's how it should be. If saving ourselves is impossible, believing in ourselves is almost as difficult.

Personally, nobody held out that "crumb of faith" which Philostratus says we should give to anyone training for a competition. I never saw it.

Maybe it's my pride, or a weakness of character, that for some silly fear of failing keeps me from sharing my most cherished projects until I've finished them with flying colors. Or because sports in general, and racing more so, have never been relevant to my conversations and interests, so that no one in my circle would ever dream to ask me what progress I was making on the track or hand me a water bottle at the end of a run.

However, I remember all too well the most common remarks whenever I did find the courage, shyly and a bit ashamed, to confide my budding enthusiasm for running. I can sum up the responses in two words: No way.

Apparently no one would stake their life on my athletic resolve the way people did for Attalus the Egyptian. They were already picturing themselves in the grave.

I don't know if it was due to their lack of faith in my muscles, so used to withering under a writing desk or bistro table, or in my mental aptitude, better trained for debating philosophy or unearthing an aorist passive from a Greek text than concentrating on a 10k through the country. Whatever the reason, the few friends who knew about my goal to become a runner saw my sudden infatuation with sports as eccentric, bewildering, maybe crazy, and definitely hopeless.

And they did right by me. Not so much for not believing in me. I wouldn't have believed in me either. If four years ago someone had told me that one day not only would I be training for a marathon but writing a book about it, I'd have burst out laughing. No, they did right by me because they gave me the best incentive there is, showing me that, first and foremost, I had to learn to place that "crumb" of faith in myself. If I now run with perseverance, I do so in large part to prove my naysayers wrong, starting with myself.

One of the most extraordinary things I've learned from running is that you have to go out and find your own motivation—with or without the unconditional faith of other people. No one can do it for you. The fans in the bleachers don't play; the players in the field do. You can't run in someone else's stead, neither to prove them wrong nor to make them proud. The solitude of the pavement is such that the fire—or water for those in the desert—must come from within. Otherwise every effort is vain and the struggle unbearable.

In fact, that outside judgment, being branded with the words "no way," became the yardstick and engine for all my training. Because it wasn't just my friends who found this running business implausible and my going through with it unlikely. It was, above all, me. I was the one who, rather than psych myself up like a Greek hero, brutally put myself down. I was the one who kept telling myself that I'd never make it, that I looked ridiculous with my glow-in-the-dark sneakers and my earbuds pumping reggaeton (which *was* and *is* ridiculous, I fear), that it was an absurd waste of time and energy, and even undignified.

Things went on like that for a while: I had zero faith in my legs, my heart, my lungs. Then, mile by mile, finish line by finish line (I still get childishly emotional when I recall the first time that I ran thirty minutes in a row), all the oily self-doubt I carried around slid away. I learned to believe in myself. I learned, with a lot of sweat and tears and persistence and determination, to trust my ability to transform every "no way" into a "yes way," at least as far as running was concerned. And this newfound faith in my abilities became a crucial motivator, which has now led me to run every day.

Philostratus should have added that to his list of motivating factors that move athletes to train. When we don't have other alternatives, we have to learn how to place that crumb of faith in ourselves. And if nobody's willing to give their life for ours, we must wring every last drop of life from our own.

S pring is slowly giving way to summer, the days are growing longer in a euphoric Paris finally freed from lockdown, the evenings all bear the promise of cocktails that bleed into dinners and dinners that bleed into nightcaps, and I've decided to go running "de bonne heure," as Proust would put it.

I can't claim to rise with the sun; I live at a latitude where the sun comes up very early. In my defense, I spend my mornings grinding out six miles, at a time when waiters in white shirts are still tidying up outdoor tables, clearing empty glasses from the night before. Despite the dark circles under my eyes, I can't complain. I love feeling my body waking with the city as I run along the Seine. I love the way my muscles, still sluggish from sleep, slowly warm up to greet the race, the passersby, the trees, the sky, and the world. Bonjour.

I'm pretty satisfied with my stamina, given the clear limitations created by my ineptitude. As for my speed, I still have work to do—a lot of work. My legs are killing me, and in the evening, before collapsing on the couch, I'm stricken with cramps, too.

Once a week I sacrifice myself to the altar of "intervals," a training technique called fartlek. This Swedish word (literally "speed play") stands for a sequence of sprints at different strides and intensities, normally aimed at improving one's speed. Northern Europeans may have been the first to perfect this technique for optimizing your running time while taking your normal route, but by now it's clear to everyone that training in intervals is the best, and only, means to learn to run faster.

Laboring to meet that objective, the other day I discovered an exercise that, hard as it was, I not only loved but chose to export from the sidewalks and make a part of my daily routine after I've taken my sneakers off.

The training, proposed by one of the many free running apps I use like scarecrows to ward off boredom, allows me to evaluate the results of a run without being a slave or prisoner to the final time recorded by my stopwatch. Minutes and seconds are, after all, just numbers. They tell us little or nothing about the success of a run. They don't tell us whether our run was intense or little more than a walk, whether it was the best or worst run ever, whether we gave it our all or the bare minimum. When it comes to running, numbers lose the universal values they hold in math, because they're relative to each runner's performance. Running a marathon in three and a half hours would be nothing short of miraculous for me. For Eliud Kipchoge, it'd be a humiliating failure.

Fartlek involves running at different levels of intensity, on a personalized scale from one to ten—we're the judge of our own performance—where one corresponds to the minimum effort we're willing to put into a run and ten the maximum, total commitment, no holding back, the supreme exertion, after which you don't have an ounce of energy left.

When I finished my first session, I was surprised to discover two things. First, running below your ability doesn't mean taking it easy. On the contrary, it's hard and frustrating, like not living up to your potential. Second, even when *you're sure you're giving it your all and then some, there is always room to push harder and go farther. When you just can't go on, you can in fact go on.*

Running, I realized that I ought to be much more patient with my muscles while warming up, when I can't hit above a four or five on the RPE scale, and that I shouldn't listen to the panicked voice in my head telling me I'm too slow and that this run will be a disaster. I want to learn to let myself run naturally instead of making myself do it by brute force. I also had proof that my regular stride is decent, that there's no point in chastising myself and piling on unnecessary pressure. I can enjoy the run, the landscape, the Seine (and my beloved podcasts about Napoleon, this year's obsession). Finally, I came to the sad conclusion that what to my mind is a titanic effort, the ceiling of my strength, a ten, for my legs doesn't score above an eight. And therefore, instead of freaking out about them, I must trust my ankles and calves. Instead of stopping them, I must give them free rein. Instead of worrying that any minute I'll collapse, I must let them do their all.

In the weeks following my spring training, I tried to apply this same exercise to all my days, starting in the morning, rating them on an intensity scale from one to ten, from the minimum effort to total dedication, entirely dependent on my own judgment (and on my goodwill, ultimately, since the judge and jury of my physical and emotional energies is me), paying no heed to the pressures of my daily organizer filled with impending deadlines and social commitments.

I have the impression that the exercise has somehow worked. At least I think it has. Though my day-to-day workload and obligations haven't changed, my stress level has gone down, a lot. So, on the most intense personal and/or professional days, I do everything in my power to give more.

Not more time, but more of myself. And in the evening, no matter how my day went, I can honestly say I'm satisfied, proud, grateful. On quieter, more relaxed days, I have to endeavor not to overdo things, to strive less and worry less, and derive from them a sense of calm and being in the moment.

In the end, running has also taught me that intensity, high or low, is worth nothing if you don't practice restraint. That, on the road or in life, giving too little of yourself is as great a risk as giving too much. That excess in any form is damaging, but so is merely surviving or living at sub-capacity; there's no point in saving your energy. And that, ultimately, whatever happens, the final judge of any race or project or relationship is us; we alone know if we could have done more or should have given less.

Running has become an awakening for me, then. And a sacred promise to keep myself honest.

III
A WAR OF ENDURANCE

I'm preparing for a marathon and don't know what I'll do with all the running skills I've gained by diligently training.

Sure, I'm learning to stick it out, to keep focused and move my legs for long distances in the hopes of getting my photo snapped at the Panathenaic Stadium and a tin medal with my name on it, but to what end?

Should I succeed in crossing the finish line at the Athens Marathon, the minute after I won't do anything with all this running and endurance.

Not because I'm planning on giving it up for good after reaching the stated aim of this book, that wouldn't be true. But because for me the point of running isn't to get from one physical place to another. No living soul has forced me to run to a place or escape from one. I don't run to get places. Most of the time my route is circular, my starting point identical to my end point. If moving is the goal, I know countless means of transportation beside my calves, scooters included. This is the 2020s, after all.

Like the large majority of runners in the Western world, I am one of those people who runs for the sake of running. I don't care about the natural reasons for running, to quickly get from one place to another as in the old saying, "Don't run!" Nor do I intend to benefit from it. I don't need to.

I'm like one of those people who loves to cook but isn't hungry enough to taste her own recipe, who learns a language for its musicality without ever having the chance to speak it with anyone. It's for the same absurd reasons and absent any clear need—which fact would send a shiver up the spine of any man or woman, not just in ancient Greece but up until three or four generations ago—that I intend to use the strength of my legs to cover twenty-five miles just for the fun, or pain, of it.

That's not always the case, at least not everywhere. There are places where people still run because they have to. And when they don't have to, they stop and rest. Take, for example, the Tarahumara, a group of legendary runners in Mexico's Sierra Madre, who can cover eighty miles a day and are venerated and studied by every ultra-marathoner in the world. But the Tarahumara only run because they have to. Generally speaking, they run to survive. They run to reach a destination, to hunt, to carry messages to places that can't be accessed by any means of transport other than a pair of legs. But when they don't have to run, they stay put and worship their gods. They wouldn't dream of organizing impossible ultramarathons just to test their superhuman stamina and hearts of steel which enable them to withstand the stifling heat of the Sierras.

Honestly, no matter how noble and mythic and glorious my motivations, I'm willing to run a marathon *for nothing at all*.

If I may say so, this is because evidently I belong to a lucky generation in a tiny portion of the world that can afford to squander an extraordinary number of calories, an equally extraordinary number of hours needed to train, as well as the money to pay for traveling to a race, registration fees, and sports equipment, all for the fun of it.

A pleasure born of a clear lack of need. I'm not even sure that, in the midst of a catastrophic urgency, my legs would heed my commands the way they do every morning along the breezy, elegant banks of the Seine. I'm even less sure that my speed and coordination would be superior to those of another human in the throes of panic.

To make this already disturbing paradox worse, I am fine with running for the sake of running, and I am fine with losing, too. I'm absolutely certain that I will suffer defeat on the day of the marathon. That's the case for nearly all runners, who gladly sign up for a race they know they can't win.

* * *

Winning, losing.

Those are the abiding rules of the game, in life as in sports.

One person raises a trophy in the air while next to them another person looks down at their mud-caked shoes, their hands empty and their eyes filled with tears. From the Trojan War to the latest local tourney, the merciless alternation of victory and defeat is the grammar of every competition. Some are left standing and others retreat into the shadows. Some can finish the task and others remain a step, or a mile, behind.

For some absurd reason that doesn't matter in footraces. Running, at least amateur running, the kind practiced by nearly all of us lifelong amateurs, the only bruised up sponsors of our energies, represents the exception to the timeless division between victory and defeat.

No one signs up for a marathon to win. And, in a way, no one ever loses either. As Emil Zatopek says, "If you want to win something, run the 100-meter dash. If you want to enjoy a real experience, run a marathon."

Aside from professional runners, those who belong to clubs or federations or teams, almost all modern marathon runners who sign up for a race—which at this point can be found in almost every inch of the globe (France alone has 7,000 a year)—have no ambition to arrive in first place or even, most likely, the top hundred. Similarly, an outcome that would be an unprecedented disgrace in any other sport—coming in five hundredth place or worse—is felt to be a triumph, something to celebrate with medals, certificates, and photographs. A galactic distance between the winner and the army of the defeated, elsewhere considered appalling, something to be erased from memory, is, in running, not only appreciated and esteemed, but honored. Kind of like the scene in *Alice in Wonderland* when the Dodo organizes a preposterous race in which every bizarre character is permitted to cross the finish line when and where they feel like, and therefore no one and everyone wins.

Furthermore, running is the one sport in the world in which, in the same competition, you'll find Olympic champions and world record holders lined up at the starting line next to amateurs of every age, provenance, physical condition, and level of training. It's entirely possible that at the London or New York marathon, on the same morning and the same pavement, number one will cross paths with number one thousand. To give you a better idea of this anomaly: picture seven-time-Golden-Ball-winner Lionel Messi standing on the soccer pitch next to a klutz like me.

And yet it stands to reason that everyone who doesn't come in first place, be it for a marathon or any other sport, is considered a loser—beaten, lapped, vanquished. Being proud of your epic spiritual win, of your private triumph over the monsters in your head, of your personal best (not, obviously, compared to anyone else's time) is all well and good, yet on the official certificate it's written in bold letters: if you didn't come in first, you belong among the losers, beyond a shadow of a doubt. But I challenge anyone to find a runner who feels like a failure after going 26.2 miles, even if it took them twenty-four hours to finish the race. Almost every long-distance runner, even the one who comes in last, feels like a Greek hero on the brink of immortal glory. And they have every right to feel that way, to hold their head high.

In short, running is a sport where few people win and the many who lose remain convinced of their own victory.

I became aware of this discrepancy between the outcomes of a race and the rules governing other sports when one day, almost laughing off the peculiar thought, I realized that in the best of cases, at *my* Athens Marathon, there would be an athlete who came in first in a third of my own time. And it didn't bother me at all.

I'd even forgotten that, for the handful of professional runners kissed at birth by the patron saint of running, there actually exists the unbelievable possibility of not only enjoying the fact that you have miraculously reached that finish line, endowed with enormous stamina and in spectacular shape, but of literally winning a marathon, of arriving at the finish line first, alone.

Running upsets the natural order of things, the permanent divide between winners and losers. What I found disturbing at first later intrigued me. Because if there's no such thing as victory and defeat in the amateur race that all of us practice, then there must be something else.

Finally, I understood. Elsewhere, off the track, those who can ignore the outcomes of their endeavors and take no interest in victory and defeat are usually kings or gods. Or children, who sense the playful side of games and don't suffer from competitiveness.

In fact, the way we run for the pleasure of running rather than to win or only to win a completely private, intangible trophy not subject to proof is a luxury. Being indifferent to the laurels of victory and the disgrace of defeat, and focusing on private achievements, on personal thresholds of success or failure that lie outside the strict rules of the game (coming in first or coming in last), indicate that running has long avoided the need for winners and losers.

That void has been replaced with a privilege: we run, *a lot*, for our own fancies and whims, for reasons that are totally private. And it is for this same taste for the superfluous that we celebrate no matter the outcome.

Our way of running lacks urgency—the urgency to win and not lose. The ancients would say what's missing from the equation is the threat of war.

* * *

What I said a moment ago about the temperament of athletes comes from modern sports, for ancient athletes were not concerned with temperament, only strength training. Some of the ancients trained by carrying massive weights, some by racing horses or rabbits. Some bent and straightened thick bars of wrought iron, others yoked themselves to wagon-drawing oxen or wrestled bulls and, incredibly, lions . . .

These ancient athletes bathed in rivers and springs, slept on the ground or on leather hides or in fields they harvested themselves. Their diet consisted of *maza* (a primitive barley cake) and unsifted, unleavened bread. They ate cow, bull, goat, and deer meat. They lathered themselves in oleaster and olive oil to prevent diseases and slow down the ravages of old age.

Some participated in as many as eight consecutive Olympiads, others nine, and they were expert handlers of heavy weaponry. They competed against each other to conquer fortresses and they were not inferior in military combat. Indeed, they were deemed worthy of trophies for their strength.

They turned warfare into athletic training, and athletic training into warfare.

This passage from Philostratus about the training of ancient athletes seems taken straight from the official website of a modern ultra-trail competition in the desert or an Ironman in the Amazon, yet it is striking for the clarity with which it sets out the basic logic undergirding every type of training, be it modern or contemporary, physical or intellectual. If we train, which is to say regularly and diligently perform a specific set of exercises, it must be for an end other than exercise.

In ancient times—which were already ancient in the age of Philostratus, who deplored his contemporary athletes for being lazy, or *argòi* in the Greek, in the absence of glorious military campaigns known to the likes of Achilles and Hector—sports were essentially considered a form of preparing for war, and vice versa.

Schools don't assign homework for the pleasure of solving equations or translating hexameters; they assign homework so that we will learn how to think for ourselves and be in the world. That's the long-term goal. The short or ultrashort-term goal is to pass the test. There's barely an adult in their right mind who, free to choose, would work without being financially compensated so they can lead the life they want. And if no soccer player would spend weeks dribbling the ball on the sidelines unless they planned to play in a match, it comes as an even greater shock that there is no concrete goal in modern fitness, that we train just to run and reject or totally ignore the fruits of our labors.

There are precisely fifty-four grueling workouts between me and the Athens Marathon (or many more, depending on how willing I am to commit to running at the expense of everything else that for brevity's sake I'll call life). That makes a total of eighteen weeks, almost four and a half months. Only then, after covering nearly three hundred miles of parks and sidewalks in Paris, in every sort of weather, will I finally be able to claim that I'm ready. Ready for what? Ready to run again.

Si vis pacem, para bellum. If you want peace, prepare for war. So goes a Roman saying attributed to the writer Vegetius, though Cicero said more or less the same thing before him. To prepare, from the Latin *prae* (first) and *parare* (to get ready or be ready).

So what are we modern runners, dedicated to the sport and committed to our workouts, getting ready for?

In the passage above, Philostratus answers with extreme clarity: the ancients, who long before the creation of the Olympics in 776 BC drew a distinction between practicing sports and spontaneously moving our bodies, thought of sports as preparation for war. People trained regularly so that one day they'd be ready to face their enemy. In fact, going into battle was intrinsically connected to sports, because the latter was a product of war. However, athletic valor surpassed military valor, since war may teach us to be brave, but, in addition to bravery, sports teach us values and, most importantly, restraint.

Legend has it that Jason, the leader of the Argonauts, founded the first pentathlon—from *āthlong* (competition) and the prefix *pénte* (five)—a competition that combines intense physical activities (wrestling, the discus throw) and lighter events (the javelin throw, the long jump, running). The first to be crowned winner of the event was Peleus, the father of Achilles, because, writes Philostratus, "he was considered the most skillful warrior among his contemporaries for the valor that he showed on the battlefield and his aptitude in the pentathlon."

This concept of sports as preparation for battle remained central to the classic conception of athletics and its organization into competitions and official disciplines. In ancient Greece, the most noble sports event was long believed to be racing in armor, a tradition in the city of Plataea in Boeotia, given how far the athletes had to run while wearing protective gear that stretched to their feet, not unlike the kind they wore into real combat.

In *On the Art of Gymnastics,* Philostratus goes on to describe being told in various cities that this form of racing began when a soldier returning from battle and still clothed in armor entered the Olympic stadium to deliver the news that they had defeated the Medes. A story our philosopher deemed credible.

That's not all. For Philostratus, footracing in general closely resembled the beginning of a battle: the athlete taking his position, the official announcing the start of the race, the horn summoning runners to form a line as if they

were an army, the signal—today a starter pistol—that literally commands athletes to start running and not stop. The
start of a race is nothing less than the onset of war.

If a speed race, commonly known as a sprint, resembles the beginning of war, then endurance running can be
seen as the end of war. Prelude not to peace, perhaps, but
at least to a temporary truce. As I said at the start of this
book, at the first marathon in history, the poor messenger
Philippides didn't schlep twenty-five miles from Marathon
to Athens to show off his physical prowess or transcend
some spiritual limits, but for a concrete military reason. He
was bearing news of the Greeks' victory and the surrender
of their enemy, the Persians, and therefore news that the
peace they yearned for had been restored.

But most modern runners are lucky to live in times of
peace.

Assuming we can trust in the durability of our geopolitical system, no one will ever ask us to run in armor that
stretches to our feet or carry messages of war across an arid
plain. Yet if millions of us flood the streets and parks of
our cities every day to run rather than take advantage of
the political harmony and social and cultural wellbeing that
we were blessed to be born into, that means that we really
aren't, deep down, at peace.

In *The Laws*, Plato writes that what most men call peace
is nothing but a name, and that in reality, by the laws of
nature, we're always at war. And there's no doubt that were
the Ancients to see us submitting to intense workout routines, sacrificing sleep and the pleasures of dining, skipping
out on parties and forms of amusement, working to the
point of exhaustion to run six or more miles a day, they'd
say we were all preparing for a war.

As I write these words, no sworn enemy is invading our national borders, at least not at the moment. So, if the danger isn't from without, it must be from within, under our chiseled muscles and stretched tendons. Combatting *that* enemy is why our runners do nothing but run. *That* is our war.

An inescapable war of endurance against the current pervasive state of wellbeing.

* * *

People don't run to fight. A marathon, if run, is above all an act of endurance.

To endure. As in to never succumb to the nagging desire to give up. To soldier on, to continue moving your legs for no other reason than to prove to yourself and others that you are determined to keep going.

It bears repeating: twenty-five miles is a considerable distance. Accustomed to running in the comforting parks of my city, where I often forget how long I've been running as I pass the pretty flowerbeds, statues, and fountains, I have a hard time picturing myself intently traveling—all in one go, I hope, without stopping—roughly the same distance that separates Milan from Bergamo or Paris from Fontainebleau.

Now regarded as the most distinguished of footraces, a competition that cannot be avoided by runners who feel compelled to say that they've completed it at least once in their lives, marathons weren't run in ancient times.

True, endurance was considered a duty in times of war. But in times of peace it was seen as completely superfluous. Olympic athletes weren't forced to prove their ability to last longer. If anything, the challenge was to be "greater" than all those who were not admitted into the stadium in search of glory.

Reading Philostratus' *Gymnastics*, I was struck—no, shocked—by how brief ancient races were. Even the races that the ancients called long were laughably short by today's standards.

In fact, not only was no one interested in endurance, not only was it not rewarded, but, in the absence of external motivating factors, like war or an emergency, it was seen as a form of madness. Anyone who dreamed of repeating the long, legendary trail of good Philippides no doubt had a screw loose.

Among the different running events hosted at the Olympic Games, Philostratus lists the simple race (a speed race), the long race (*dòlichos*), the race in armor, and the double-stadion race, called the diaulos, from the Greek *dís* (twice) and *aulós* (stadion).

The legends surrounding the origins of each of these races reveal how for the Greeks endurance was beside the point.

> The origin of the dolichos, or long race, is as follows: couriers frequently traveled between Arcadia and Greece proper to deliver messages concerning war. Going by horse was forbidden, so they had to run. This led to the habit of running, for training purposes, as many stades [600 feet, first measured by the foot of Hercules; the stadium in Olympia was two hundred yards long] as the *dolichos* [twenty-four stades in Olympia, or roughly three miles long], the distance of today's long race, which turned them into real runners and readied them for war.
>
> The stadion, or simple race, was invented by the Eleans, who, when they made ritual sacrifices, placed all their sacred

objects upon an altar but did not immediately set fire to them. Bearing torches, the runners would line up one stade away from the altar, where the priest stood and acted as the umpire. The winner of the race, having gotten there first, would light the fire and walk away from the altar with the Olympic crown.

After the Eleans had made their sacrifices, any envoys from other parts of Greece who were present were also required to make an offering. So that their own approach to the altar was worthy of note, the runners ran away from the altar as if inviting the Greeks to sacrifice [*tò Hellenikòn*] and then ran back again to show that the Greeks would be glad to come. That was the origin of the double-stadion race.

Philostratus goes on to say that until the XIII Olympiad the only official competition was the simple, stadion-long race, which no runner ever won twice. (It's astounding to think that so important were sports in ancient Greece that time was counted in Olympiads, every four years, beginning with the first Olympics in 776 BC, hence the XIII Olympiad would have been held fifty-two years after, in 724 BC.) The double-stadion race was added later, followed by the long race, the first winner of which was Acanthus of Sparta.

So, the longest running event in the ancient world didn't even top three miles.

I'd never have thought that the brief little recovery runs I take to catch my breath and cool down my muscles, trotting around and listening to podcasts, would have made me an Olympic athlete in Ancient Greece. I'm not sure whether I should be proud and add the dolichos to my currently barren trophy case or remain baffled by the twenty-five-mile-long marathon that awaits me, an endurance race almost nine times longer than what the ancients regarded as a long run.

And it doesn't end there. The marathon, a distance which for me remains insurmountable and synonymous with tremendous exertion, is considered by many runners little more than a walk in the park, an ordinary rite of passage to stretch your limbs on your way to far more epic competitions, like ultramarathons, Ironmans, and ultra trails, in this inebriated day and age that seems to demand human beings keep raising the bar.

About this subject, which I could briefly and ignorantly define as "anything that miraculously tops the effort required of a marathon" or "any race prefaced with the word ultra," I've read stories that would make your hair stand on end.

Surely it's my lack of experience and training, yet I struggle to find, I won't say alluring, but acceptable, within the bounds of all that we tend to consider human, competitions that call for running hundreds of miles across steppes and deserts, fleeing wild animals, procuring food with your bare hands, drinking from streams, or braving arctic temperatures while hoofing it in the snow.

I sort of understand triathlons, even if they're not my bag. Swimming 2.8 nautical miles, cycling 112 miles, and finishing it off with a cool marathon: it's the perfect combination to be able to call yourself an immortal, or almost.

The pentathlon was created by Jason three thousand years ago. The triathlon, on the other hand, wasn't established until 1977, under the Hawaiian sun, on a friendly bet. Arguing over the toughest endurance event in Honolulu—a roughwater swim, an up- and downhill run, or a long bike race—Navy Commander John Collins suggested combining all three into one outrageous sports event that would take the name Ironman, since anybody strong or crazy enough to finish them back-to-back was a man made of iron. And the women?

Only fourteen contenders showed up for the first Ironman. One of them had bought his first racing bike the day before. Another took long breaks between each leg to fuel up at a fast-food restaurant. Forty-five years later, the triathlon is today one of the most coveted endurance events in the world. In the US, the name Ironman is a registered trademark, and thousands of athletes are willing to do anything to suffer in the most inhospitable and spectacular corners of the planet, including Murakami, who in the final chapter of *What I Talk About When I Talk About Running* recounts with a mix of horror and passion his tenacious drive to finish the triathlon on a Japanese island.

The Latin expression *non plus ultra* seems not to apply to today's endurance-obsessed runners, who can never get their fill of pushing their physical limits, so that now most major sports labels have turned "no limits" into a kind of calling card, nurturing the illusion that, wherever you set it, a limit is no more than a minor detail to overcome.

Generally speaking, an ultramarathon is any footrace exceeding the distance between the cities of Athens and Marathon. The list of current Herculean runs that surpass 26.2 miles is long—and pretty intimidating for common mortals who feel like champions after running a local half marathon.

The most famous—and grueling for the training it takes to run and its extreme temperatures—is the Marathon des Sables, also known as "the expedition race" in the Sahara Desert. Participants must run 150 miles in just six days, with some legs exceeding fifty miles a day, while carrying their own provisions (though fortunately not their own water), in weather conditions that include sandstorms, suffocating heat, and all-day humidity. Every year more than a thousand enthusiasts are drawn to the Marathon des Sables.

Another well-known, insanely ambitious ultramarathon is the Yukon Arctic Ultra, which foists upon athletes a 430-mile course in northern Canada, where the temperatures range from fourteen to -4 degrees Fahrenheit. Carrying their provisions on their back, of course. It's even more challenging than Napoleon's invasion of Russia, making it perhaps the hardest course in the world. But there are many others, too. The Trans 555+ Elite Runners Race, a course hundreds of kilometers long under the Egyptian pyramids. The Jungle Marathon in the middle of the Brazilian Amazon. The Barkley in Tennessee, where runners retrace the route of an escaped prisoner on a course with 54,200 feet of accumulated vertical climb. Then there's the Deca-Ironman in Monterrey, an Ironman times ten! I even discovered there's such a thing as the Spartathlon, a 153-mile-long ultramarathon from Athens to Sparta modeled on the first legendary run of Philippides. Such extreme races may be fodder for another book, but it's not one I intend to write.

However, partly due to the frequent number of serious and fatal accidents, people are beginning to question events like these, which push the boundaries of what's possible to the point of risking the lives of their participants and seem to defy the Olympic spirit in their desire to rid their courses of aid stations. Events that are in essence more like gambling with your life than competing in a sport.

It was more than a little disturbing—I'll never forget the chill that bore through me—to hear the news of twenty-one Chinese long-distance runners dying of hypothermia in May

2021, when they were caught by surprise by hailstorms and freezing rains during an ultramarathon in the mountains of the Yellow River Stone Forest in northern China. Survivors said that conditions were so bad that they couldn't stand up along the crevices.

Given my own puny training regimen, I don't really know what to say about such an inexplicable, almost intoxicating need to keep pushing oneself. But I think I know what the Greeks would call it: *hybris*.

In ancient Greek *hybris* was an idea with serious moral implications. It might be translated as "excessiveness," an arrogant attitude toward nature and the limits it imposes, the opposite of temperance, moderation, and an awareness of oneself and one's limits.

"See how lightning falls on the highest buildings and tallest trees, because heaven brings low all things that surpass greatness," writes Herodotus in *Histories* (Book 7, 10). *Hybris* was synonymous with craven behavior, small-mindedness, the inability to accept the human condition which, compared to the perfect and immortal condition of deities, is limited, negligible.

For the Greeks, when it came to sports, perseverance may have been beside the point, but overperforming was seen as a crime, an outrage, an inability to be human through and through.

The physical limits set by our muscles, tendons, lungs, and heart, by our genetic wiring, could not be surpassed or raised by hard work and training. Progress was not the highest value to pursue at all costs, and it was scandalous to want to go beyond, *ultra*, the human condition. Duty and honor came from the courage to fill the gap between our limitations with remarkable feats and the laurels of glory.

In short, an athlete who stretched his body *ultra* its limits was not greeted by the sound of cheers in the stadium but by the sound of the Titans' broken nails as they crawled to the heavens and were immediately driven back down by Zeus.

* * *

One wonders what the prize for all our running and persevering is. What's the trophy? The final payoff?

Personally, I have no idea. I struggle to picture my soul swelling with pride because of a crown of laurels or with a feeling of victory at the end of the Athens Marathon. At most I'll be able to feel I've won in the proud gaze of the person I love and who I hope will be waiting for me at the finish line. But I have the sensation that after I've run twenty-five miles my life won't be any different. I don't see there being any awards at the end of the race, certainly no more than a photo to preserve the memory, and I fear that the fact of completing a marathon will quickly wind up becoming a footnote in my biography, swallowed up by my daily chores, by work, home, family, and by new, stark-raving mad, physical and intellectual adventures to be undertaken.

What's more, I worry that my happiness about reaching the finish line won't last long and that, absent any real prizes, the glory of running a marathon will turn out to be much more fleeting than I'd always imagined.

The Italian word "*agonismo*," which refers to an athlete's competitive spirit, to his or her effort to excel during an event, and therefore by extension to the professional side of sports—comes from the Greek word *agonismòs,* struggle. The word itself can be broken down further: into agon, a generic competition, from the Greek verb *ágo*, meaning to push, lead, or command.

Few eras in history were as shamelessly competitive, I think, as that of ancient Greece, when nearly everything was a contest, an agon, from battles to sports, from art to rhetoric. And the one prize for every physical and intellectual struggle was a handful of immortal verses.

Ever since Homer's *Iliad*, it was a given that war would be immortalized in verse. Yet I think many runners would be at least as shocked as I was to find out that the ultimate prize at the Olympics—the meaning behind all that sweat, training, and determination—was a poem.

That is precisely why, after centuries of songs about the deeds of immortal deities, it was in the West that there emerged the first poetic genre dedicated to the deeds of men, including their athletic achievements. You might even go so far as to say that nonreligious poetry is partly a product of sports, and vice versa, because the one was established at the same time as the other, in the seventh century BC, shortly after the founding of the Olympic games. After Homer enshrined the grand collective ideals, the time had come to glorify the individual, first name and last, whose excellence in the stadium rendered Greece great no longer by his skill in battle, not exclusively anyway, but by his muscles.

The ancients called this genre lyric poetry because it was always accompanied by the lyre, as we can see in the illustrations on Greek vases which can be admired in museums today. The lyric was further divided into monodic poems (sung by one person) and choral poems (performed by a chorus).

Of the writing devoted to those once-in-a-lifetime moments—births, weddings, funerals—one genre stands out: the epinicion, a choral lyric celebrating the winners of games, known in Greek as *epiníkion*, meaning *epí* (above) and *níke* (victory), combined with *mélos* (song), or victory song. Arranged in three parts, an epinicion describes the athlete's victory, his personal story and the story of his ancestors, a mythological part and a concluding moral padded with maxims and precepts. Recited during the many banquets that followed sports events in antiquity, the poems were commissioned by the victor and his family from a poet of their choosing, not unlike the way we hire a photographer to immortalize the moments we want to remember.

Among the authors of epinicions that have made it down to us, mention must be made of Simonides, Bacchylides, and Pindar. The latter was the indisputable champ of praising athletes and the proponent of a stylistic ambiguity that borders on the enigmatic. Thanks to Pindar, we know the feats—or performances, as we'd say today, the personal bests—of many ancient athletes, as well as the immense pride their families took in them. One standout is Arcesilaus II of Cyrene, winner of the 466 BC chariot race who figures prominently in Pindar's longest epinicion in existence, Pythian IV.

In other words, in ancient Greece there was just one way for human beings to lay claim to the first-person singular, to say "I" and separate themselves from the pack, and that way was to excel at sports and in exchange receive a poem.

The English word "record" refers, among other things, to what must be set down so as not to be forgotten. The Greeks placed their faith in the immortality of the poetic act. Who knows what we believe, we modern, uncompetitive runners, so spoiled with wellbeing that we run without a thought of winning and are, as a result, bereft of rewards that can capture forever the moment that we cross the finish line.

Call me romantic or old-fashioned, but a handful of poetic lines still strikes me as being an excellent reason to run your heart out. I won't rule out asking for some for myself once I've completed my marathon in Athens. It's an excellent way to protect the personal war of endurance that is long-distance running—to protect it from being trivialized, from oh, what the heck. From silence.

I felt like a change of scenery this morning, so I ditched the bottle-green Seine for the lush, early-summer flowerbeds in the Jardin des Plantes. Happy to run amid the fragrant grass, red gerberas, and daisies, while I was giving thanks for the fresh air and promising start to the day, I suddenly realized that this was the place, right here, between this elegant Parisian garden and the long boulevard de l'Hôpital next to it, where three years ago I became a runner.

It wasn't the memory of the outrageous, almost superhuman exertion of those first workouts that struck me this morning. (I'm not exaggerating when I say that starting to run was the hardest challenge that I have ever undertaken. I perfectly recall those first, futile efforts every time I strap on my running shoes: how my knees burned and calves quaked, how close I was, after just a few feet into a run, to bursting into tears on the street.) No, what disturbed me this morning was the nagging thought that I don't know why, one fine day, I took up running.

Until now I'd never asked myself why I decided to take up running rather than, say, climbing or tennis or dance, or any of the thousand sports invented by man. It had nothing to do with habit or experience; running isn't a "family affair," as Cecile Coulon writes in her memoir Petit éloge du running. For Coulon, running came naturally, because her parents and *siblings ran with the same regularity with which someone else might read books or go to the movies. As a child, I never saw a pair of running shoes at home, nor, at other times in my life, did running rear its head, not even remotely. My friends don't run, and my world, the world of culture, rarely talked about sports or jaunts in the woods.*

So when, in recent years, I started to run along the Seine, I wasn't trying to emulate anyone, nor was I prompted by someone's having sung, even faintly, its praises. What came over me? Thinking about it now, as I train for a marathon, the least natural and least spontaneous of pastimes, I get the impression that throwing myself into running was a straight-forward matter. My ineptitude aside, the decision to run was organic, the only available option. I didn't ponder which among the many sports to take up; my first and only intu- ition was to run. Faithfully, I heeded its call. I wanted to rouse my soft body and tired spirit. Running was the only conceivable choice. And still is. Even now that I'm quick and in shape, even now that not a weekend has gone by in the last three years when I haven't been exercising, I remain de- voted to running, I wouldn't dream of dropping it for another sport. Like Murakami, I'd be terrified of losing the more than modest gains I've made with all my sweat and training. If I continue to run, it is to honor the hard work I've done to get where I am.

Spontaneity and a lot of pride. Too much pride. That's what really led me to running. Given what miserable shape I was in, I'd never have set foot in a gym or jogged out into a field to partake in an instructor-led course and endured the gazes of people in better shape than me. Running doesn't re- quire explanations or lessons; you don't go to running school.

*You learned how to walk as a child, I must have told myself
unconsciously, now all you need to do is pick up the pace.
Also, running is, by definition, a solitary sport. Even in a
group you're on your own, because in the end, your legs,
head, and heart are yours alone and can't be penetrated.
For at least the first year I said absolutely nothing to anyone about this personal revolution of mine, and because they
were secret those twenty or thirty minutes of being winded
gave me more pleasure, and more strength. To this day I am
adamant about running alone, inventing excellent excuses to
avoid going running with my partner, a real long-distance
runner in much better shape than me.*

    *I often wonder what else draws me to this asphyxiating
activity of endless staying power, aside from its being a sport
for lone wolves. It must be admitted that there aren't many
sports as boring, at least on paper, as running. It isn't fun and
games. There are no balls, no boundaries, no teammates, no
bodies of water to wade in or mountains to climb and take
in the view. In fact, all there is to do when you run is control
your breath and place one foot in front of the other for miles.*
    *Four million years ago, in Ethiopia, our species evolved to
stand erect on two feet and no longer crawl on all fours, not
by instinct or because of the surrounding environment but in
order to run. Human beings discovered they could walk up-
right by running, slowly but for long stretches. What humans
lost in speed, they gained in endurance. One of the oldest
forms of hunting, which gave our species greater nourish-
ment and improved our mental faculties, is called persistence
hunting, a practice of running patiently behind prey that,
though much faster, has less stamina than humans, until it
collapses from exhaustion.*

All evidence points to the fact that my attitude toward running confirms the soundness of this evolutionary theory. My daily runs are an exercise in persistence, only in my case the prey is me, as well as my physical and mental equilibrium. In my life I have sought wellbeing, good cheer, and calm—a state of peace, generally, or at least an armistice— by any means (most of them legal). None produced better results, and lasted longer, with no aftereffects or exorbitant costs, than running. Like my fellow hominids of yore, I ultimately realized that all I need to do is pursue what I want. If I can last long enough, it will eventually fall at my feet. That's why I like endurance so much: because there has yet to be a bad mood or pain that hasn't melted away after a half-hour run.

Just imagine what running six miles regularly for three years can do, I thought this morning in the Jardin des Plantes. In the end, you stop walking and start moving faster just to outrun whatever's ailing you: to defy it, to dominate it, to make it see who's in command. Once again, thanks to running, today I can say I've won. At least until tomorrow.

IV
TAMING TIME:
KAIROS, FLOW, AND THE PRESENT MOMENT

A minute means little, next to nothing.

Yet were I to count the number of minutes I've let slip through my fingers, not hearing them tick by because I was busy doing something else—or more often than not thinking about something other than their passing—they'd add up to years.

Then I started running. And from that moment on I felt the physicality of time surge up inside me—necessary, painful, shocking.

Practically speaking, if someone asked you to wait "a couple minutes," that handful of seconds would be no big deal, one of thousands of occasions where you could, for example, fish your phone out of your pocket and let yourself be hypnotized, like a stunned snake, scrolling through your feed of choice until you forgot time altogether. Try running "a couple minutes" and you'll be able to touch time's dusty curtain, which is forever falling on things and life.

I don't think it's really a matter of a minute seeming to drag on when we're hard at work and flying unpityingly away when we're taken up with something pleasant and lighthearted, *fugit inreparabile tempus*, as Virgil says in the *Georgics*. I've often had the impression while running that I'm piercing the surface of why the minute-and-hour hand turn and finding myself somewhere else, somewhere inside that progression of seconds and minutes and weeks and years which we call time.

I no longer cared about arresting (as if!) those hands. Suddenly the box containing all the innerworkings of clocks had flung open.

What I felt with astonishment, curiosity, fear and, once again, shock, wasn't quite connected to the passage of time (which always passes) as I prayed for it to be over soon so that I could finally remove my running shoes and rest, bringing an end to my animal suffering. At some point I wasn't even aware of its passing, as if by running I had stepped behind the clear demarcations that we usually imagine time having, which inevitably divide it into past, present, and future, and I found myself in the outrageous position of bearing witness to the matter of which it's made, to the heft of it.

For me, this was a Copernican revolution. I stopped my demented struggle to avoid the cage of time in which we're permanently trapped by the laws of physics. And for the first time I began to look around me, to understand what exactly lies inside that prison and whether some good could come from it, despite our being its prisoners.

In short, after a lifetime of agonizing about what time is, thanks to running I was liberated from this inescapable, crudely Proustian obsession and quickly turned to another obsession. I wanted to know what's inside time.

* * *

Now that I'd figured out the question, I had to try to look for an answer.

Obviously, all I came up with were more questions. And an idea, a Greek one. Maybe the door to the dimension of time, which running had thrown open before my blundering, was no other than the Greek concept of *kairós*, that critical moment or time out of time that, evidently, I had never fully appreciated.

In the fourth century BC, the last great sculptor of classical Greece, Lysippos, who had also worked at the court of Alexander the Great, made a bronze statue he called, simply, Kairos. The sculpture did not survive the centuries, so today all we know it by are inferior, subsequent copies and poets' descriptions of it. Among the most striking are the verses of Posidippus, a Macedonian epigrammist who turned Lysippos's Kairos into a metaphor and warning about the opportunities time offers for those capable of grasping it.

Here he is imaging a dialogue between time and man, in words that some sources believe were carved into the original statue:

> "Who are you?"
> "I'm Kairos, lord of the world."
> "Why do you walk on the tips of your toes?"
> "Because I never stop running."
> "Why do you have wings on your feet?"
> "Because I fly like the wind."
> "Why are you holding a razor in your right hand?"
> "To show men that I, Kairos, am sharper than any edge."
> "Why does your hair hang over your face?"
> "So he who meets me can grab me, by Zeus."
> "Then why is the back of your head bare?"
> "Because once my winged feet have carried me off no one can catch me from behind, no matter how desperately they desire to."
> "And why did the artist make a sculpture of you?"
> "For you mortals, stranger. And he set me in the doorway to warn you."

Copy that, Lysippos.

Now I know that before putting on my running shoes I did nothing but chase after time, begging it to stand still when I was happy and fly by when I was suffering. I was always behind it, staring at the bare back of its head, and all the while I kept slamming my head, and my brain, against the sharp edge of the razor in his hands.

When I first started running, I found myself faced with time, though I hadn't even realized it, and he was kindly proffering his golden hair, as the poet's metaphor has it, so that I could seize him and make him mine.

Used to chasing after time, I didn't know how to reach out and grab it, with all the responsibility that entails, especially the duty to derive something good from it. I wanted to, but I didn't know how.

For a long time I stood there, bewildered. The prospect was attractive, sure, but the responsibility great. Then one day I stopped thinking about it, I cautiously held out my hand, as if I were balancing on the invisible gangplank that running had become for me, and finally I caught it by the hair. Ever since then, time has been mine.

I might not have wings on my feet, but those forty minutes of running that I like to inflict on myself have taught me, without the possibility of appeal, that you neither lose time nor gain time. You can do a thousand things at once, or nothing, but there's no such thing as a twenty-five-hour day. Or a twenty-three-hour day.

Time is either put to use or wasted, filled with meaning or emptied of it.

Having rejected the prospect of lounging on the couch, I quickly found myself faced with the problem of what to do with it, with those minutes when I insist on running. Making them speed up, so that the physical exertion passes quickly, wasn't an option. I couldn't prolong the moments I felt liberated, the moments I felt well, either. The only way I could avoid quitting was to make those minutes meaningful.

Aristotle writes that kairos is "the opportune time," or *tagatón' . . . en chróno* (*Nicomachean Ethics*, 1096a). Simpler still: kairos is how we choose to make use of time; the concrete things we choose to do with our time.

This arises from the nature of things, from their transience and the urge to respond to that transience. If time is a straight line, with a beginning and an end, kairos is a circle that expands on every point of the line that we decide to put to good use.

Kairos has long been confused—by yours truly first and foremost—with the fleeting instant, with the here-and-gone moment that you have to catch on the fly, but it has nothing to do with Horace's *carpe diem*. It isn't something that, once seized, vanishes never to be seen again.

Kairos *can* be repeated, believe me, as often as there are minutes and hours and days between the day we're born and the day we die.

Kairos is not a fixed point in time. It doesn't have a beginning and an end. Instead, it is a continuous action. The Greeks, with their sublime, punctilious conception of grammatical tense, could say it better than I can. Kairos isn't "I run" or "I won" or "I love" or "I weep." It's a kind of motion photography, its focus blurry: "I'm running," "I'm loving." All of which means, in the end, "I'm living."

Ultimately, dissecting time to figure out what it is means answering the question *when*. Whereas trying to grasp

Kairos, when and where you can, means asking *what* to do with the time you've been given, however much or little that may be.

* * *

Not that I've done great things with this unusual dimension of time that running has bestowed on me. I'm no Murakami, running in the early dawn under the snow and mentally preparing talks at Harvard.

What occupies my moments of kairos is pretty forgettable, when I'm fairly lucid and my mind isn't filled with whatever I have planned that day, with the things I have to do and the people I have to see post-run, or with the trials of the day before. As for the music I listen to while running, no comment.

But that doesn't matter. The point of becoming aware of what is, and what buzzes, inside time isn't to pass judgment on what's going through our heads. The real point is to realize that something is at least going on up there.

Even if I'm unable to fill every kairos of mine with "goodness," to paraphrase Aristotle, for me the real discovery, and the real relief, was knowing that it exists and can be accessed. That, even if we don't always have the tenacity and can-do attitude to use it, inside time there is something that transcends the fleeting nature of our days and lives. A kind of travel kit is what I mean, which we can, if we want, pack with meaning that can survive the transience of our days and remain forever, in our memory, whole and intact, just the way we left it.

At this point you'd be right to ask why it was running

in particular that gave me concrete proof that I could rub shoulders with kairos, rather than any of the other thousand activities that I happen to do every day. I asked myself the same question. What makes those forty bruising, short-winded minutes stand out from the other twenty-three hours of my day? And why an activity as trivial as running and not the nobler art of music or literature or the awe-inspiring spectacle of nature?

It took me a while to figure it out, but I think the key to everything lies in being present.

During no other endeavors that I've undertaken—with the exception of writing, on the occasional lucky day—am I so fully, totally, obstinately present as I am when I run.

In every other activity, including the most pleasurable, making love among them, I'm there, yes, sometimes I'm *very much* there, but almost never with 100% of my mental faculties. The next minute I'm distracted, thinking of the next day, squaring off against my fears, and generally transported elsewhere by the incessant flow of my thoughts. Not so when I run. I'm there, all of me is incredibly there, and I can do nothing but observe myself, whole, vulnerable, full, naked.

Maybe, in my ordinary case, it's the sweat and toil. Maybe it's some biochemical mechanism to offset the strain of my muscles by making my heart pump more blood, and therefore more oxygen, to my brain, so that suddenly the world becomes crisper, clearer. Maybe it's the absence of any form of physical distraction save for a pair of earbuds planted in my ears and my urban surroundings. Maybe it's the way my legs are summoned to give everything they've got to drive my feet forward as rapidly as possible, and every second feels like years, so one tries to the best of their ability to fill up the time, by counting sheep—there are coaches who recommend counting your footfalls to keep focused—or by losing yourself in Freudian analysis. Maybe it's the way a run is like an ancient pilgrimage: the faithful would reach such states of devotion to their chosen path that they'd become completely absorbed in their footsteps along their travels, intensifying the religious faith that had sustained them in a perfect harmony between body and spirit.

I can't think of a clear answer, but I am aware that from time to time, when I run, I approach a state of consciousness that psychologists call flow, a word coined by the Hungarian Mihaly Csikszentmihalyi to define a state of being completely immersed in an activity yet at the same time fully present. A subject of study since the 1960s, especially in sports, flow involves total focus on a goal and a powerful, innate sense of purpose, which is compensated by a sense of fulfillment for having performed a particular task.

What the English have dubbed flow and the Greeks once called kairos, Eastern philosophies refer to as total consciousness or, in the current parlance, mindfulness, present-moment thinking. To be there, in the moment. To be entirely there without trying to change or control it. Indeed, to put yourself in the hands of life, to let yourself be— simply and completely.

It would seem—I have no proof yet, but I'll find out soon enough—that the hardest part of a marathon isn't getting your muscles to work for four hours. They can do that on their own. As long as they don't have to put up with your constant inner monologue. Indeed, the trickier thing is to let yourself simply run, to allow yourself *to be* in the race, to put all your mental presence into it and ignore the voice in your head that repeats with every step: "You'll never make it!"

Moreover, runners who claim to have had an intense emotional experience while running—unexpected tears of joy, heightened perceptions, a sense of wellness not unlike ecstasy—aren't rare. Though not everyone achieves mystical levels of satisfaction (it happened to me once, and I was shocked to find myself foolishly crying in the middle of the street) running may provide the pinnacle of emotional wellbeing divorced from reason.

Psychologists call this ecstasy "peak experience," a phrase first used in 1970 by the American Abraham Maslow to refer to the maximum gratification produced by the state of flow—runner's orgasm, sort of. Once a runner comes down from this higher plane, he or she feels exhausted, undone by the emotion, the way we feel after sex, yet at the same time full of an unprecedented amount of energy.

According to cognitive scientists, the state of flow, this chance to cling so firmly to time that you penetrate it, can be experienced not only in sports but in spiritual dimensions, in education (does anyone else remember being so intensely absorbed by an idea or method that it felt more like being in a trance than hitting the books?) and, in cases that are a privilege of being, in sexuality.

I may not be qualified to say those scientists are right, but I want to say it. I've never felt as closely connected to life or in the presence of time as when I've possessed an idea or a partner.

Or as when I began running. That most of all.

* * *

To my embarrassment, it is only now, as I fret about finishing my marathon with a dignified time—about finishing it at all!—that I realize that neither *On the Art of Gymnastics* nor any other Greek text that I've read reports the finish times of athletes in ancient Greece.

Starting with the first Olympics, exactly how fast the Greek runners were isn't written anywhere, so we'll never know. What is more, given obvious technical limitations, time was pretty much ignored during ancient competitions, because it couldn't be calculated. I'd say it's rather disturbing, for an age that puts a premium on speed, in running shoes or not, to discover that time was a forgettable, superfluous detail for the ancient Greeks.

Chronometry, the science of measuring time—from Greek, no less: *chronos* (time) and *metron* (measure)—dates to ancient Egypt, when the first water clocks and colossal obelisks to track the movement of the sun were conceived. Along with sundials, hydraulic clocks were perfected in ancient Greece using increasingly sophisticated systems and eventually led to the construction of the Athens Wind Tower in the first century BC. Apparently, Plato may even have owned a kind of water-powered alarm clock to rouse his sleepy students. But no one (due to a lack of means, clearly) ever thought to time Olympic performances.

Speed wasn't what counted in ancient races. Winning did. Only the person who came in first would survive history. Everyone else was consigned to oblivion. Today, accustomed to (and occasionally spoiled by) scientific precision, we'll never know how fast the Greeks really ran. Nor will we be able to quantify their records. There's no data, just our imaginations.

It goes without saying that the absence of precision watches led to a lot of uncertainty about the results of a race. And to a lot of cheating. Philostratus attests to there having been an epidemic of wins bought with money, not earned with sweat. Sources say that during the Olympic games in 396 BC, the athlete Leon of Ambracia disputed the results of his long-distance race. Leon claimed to have come in first, but the judges pretended otherwise. Although the laurels didn't fall to him, the corrupt judges were slapped with a large fine.

From the clepsydra to the pendulum of Galileo and Newton, from mechanical clocks to electric watches, the need to measure time first arose not in sports but in sailing. Beginning in the second half of the 1700s, almanacs and trigonometric tables for ships led to the first English timepieces, which would limit the number of miscalculations and, therefore, of shipwrecks.

What prompted the refinement of measuring time in sports races was not a reverence for bursts of speed but the earnings generated by gambling. It was essential for gamblers to know exactly who won and how much money they were owed.

At the first modern Olympiad in 1896, footraces were timed with a Longines chronograph, which could measure up to a fifth of a second. That seems quite accurate, until you consider that in a hundred-meter dash a person covers at least two meters in a fifth of a second. It wasn't until the 1912 games held in Stockholm that time was first kept electronically. That was also the year that ropes separating running lanes were replaced by chalk lines, the starter pistol made its first appearance, and at the finish line the judge's timer snapped a photo to create what we now call the photo finish. Running times were measured to one tenth of a second.

The international system of units, or SI, has recognized the second as a unit of measurement since its inception in 1889, and since 1963 it has defined the second as "the duration of 9 192 631 770 periods of the radiation corresponding to the transition between two hyperfine levels of the ground state of the caesium 133 atom." Today, the main sports events are timed with atomic clocks, which can calculate wins to the hundredth and thousandth of a second, limiting human error as much as possible.

Sure, I'm no expert in physics or sports, but I'd never considered the importance of measuring time until a chance meeting with a member of the Italian Timekeepers Federation (*Federazione Italiana Cronometristi*, or FICR) who, seeing how worried I was about my time in the Athens Marathon, something I now annoy anyone in earshot about, he replied in the curt, matter-of-fact way you'd expect of a timekeeper. Having one's time measured correctly, he said, is every runner's fundamental right.

I'd never thought of that. Being able to record exactly how long it takes to finish a race is a privilege of the present day, one that athletes were denied for centuries, starting with the Greeks, or circumvented for the sake of convenience. According to this—new to me—line of reasoning, time, like all other rights, is a symptom of democracy, and therefore freedom—no longer a prison to escape from or a burden to boycott.

An athlete is only ever denied their inalienable right not when she is disqualified (you still get a time, however meaningless) but when she violates the purpose of a specific sport. In fact, in all competitions there exists a maximum time, past which a participant is no longer competing, just messing around. After the set time limit, even a Swiss time-keeper will give up on such mediocrity and decline to clock the finish time.

Now that I know it's my right, that time—and every time of my existence—I want it. I no longer worry about it, even if it's worse than others' times or different from the time I'm expecting. Actually, I plan to claim every last second of it, without cheating. The alternative would mean leaving no trace or living outside time, like a clown. Or being disqualified, like a thief.

In *Confessions*, Saint Augustine writes of time: "If no one asks me, I know what it is. If I wish to explain it, I don't know. Yet I can confidently say that I know that, if nothing were to pass away, there would be no past, and if nothing were to arrive, there would be no future, and if nothing were to be, there would be no present."

I'm not sure I can say what time really is. But I have managed to feel it when I run. That may not sound like much, but it's enough for me. And a comfort.

T he month of June has brought unseasonable rain, making my morning runs along the banks of the Seine soupy and slick, and an unexpected discovery about running that at first unsettled me and then—thanks to my bad habit of turning everything into poetry, my defects most of all—worked its charm.

A few days ago, following all the precautions my ambition to run a marathon demands, including looking after my health, I went to see a cardiologist to get what, when I was at school, we called a certificato di buona e robusta costituzione. A certificate of sound constitution. A clean bill of health. I don't remember having ever had an electrocardiogram before last Tuesday. I'd thought my heart was indestructible, like a stone, as a friend of mine likes to tease. If my heart had never stopped beating before, despite being broken more than once in this life, I don't see why it would have anything against pumping all the blood it takes to tackle a twenty-six mile stroll. And yet . . .

Apparently I have a slow heart rate—severely slow. That explains the alarm that would sometimes flash across my smartwatch, the guardian angel of my athletic efforts. The medical term is bradycardia, from ancient Greek, bradys (slow) and kardia (heart). It seems that my heart rate is far below the sixty-beat-per-minute norm. The doctor was *shocked it had never been brought to my attention before, as was I, though they say it's nothing grave. Smiling to (literally) hearten me, she concluded that I had the heart of an athlete, or a long-distance runner. Too bad I haven't run a marathon yet.*

Bradycardia, which afflicts many athletes, especially those who practice distance sports, has in fact been a subject of medical studies for a long time. They say that Fausto Coppi had a heart rate of forty beats per minute. Other long-distance athletes have had even slower heart rates. If we can't deny that playing sports anatomically modifies the heart—to endure the strain and become more effective, the cardiac muscle changes, growing in size and lowering the number of contractions at rest—than for some athletes having "a big heart" or "a crazy heart" is more than a clever saying. I never thought I'd be one of them. Nor did I think that in just three years running could change my life and my cardiac muscle so dramatically.

Who knows, I may have had bradycardia before, and all running did was intensify my genetic makeup. One thing is for sure: I often wonder what my initiation in sports has meant to my body, what this biological revolution signified for my physique, having to quickly adapt to its demands for energy, effort, and endurance—demands diametrically opposed to those it was tasked with when I was born and lived restfully for more than thirty years.

There are mornings, like today, when I run over nine miles and honestly think that if it had been up to my body alone, the CEO of all my cells, as in the cartoon about the human body we watched as kids, faced with these pretensions to athletic glory it would have told me to go to hell a long time ago. For decades accustomed not only to bad sleeping and eating habits, but to spending entire days tied to a desk, I find it incredible that, when asked to entertain this eccentric, unprecedented idea of going out for a run every day, my legs, lungs, tendons, and ankles simply said, "Okay."

Aside from some stiffness in my back and initial cramps, no doubt due to lactic acid buildup, I haven't had any running-related accidents or injuries. I'm almost afraid to write that down now and jinx my fast-approaching marathon in Athens. I hope that continues to be the case for a while. Maybe, as Murakami writes, I lucked out in the DNA department and have a body that can adapt to tests of endurance. I didn't earn it, I just had the outrageous good fortune that many people are denied. I have the general impression that my body has adapted to running much faster than my brain. In fact, after three years, my brain is still baffled by my ability to survive an hour and a half run, whereas when all is said and done my legs may find it strange but get through it without flying into hysterics.

Maybe before running I had forgotten that I possessed a body. Its physical form was not a priority. But if, a few summers ago, someone had suggested I go to bed with the chickens so that I could get up early the next day and jog twelve miles, I'd have happily injured myself to avoid what was clearly, for me, torture. My body, on the other hand, benevolent and generous beyond my wildest dreams, not only accepted this routine immediately and without objection, but it adapted to it, too, setting in motion a series of anatomical mutations that made running bearable and pleasant. Starting with my bpm.

Having ascertained that my heart, at least for the moment, isn't at risk of seizing up, I turned this discovery into a beautiful metaphor, about running and about life. My heart isn't, as some people say, lazy. It's just prudent and very, very needy.

Whatever adventure I presume to embark on, running shoes or not, my minimum and maximum are well above average, so it stands to reason that in order to give more, I have to give a lot more. And, conversely, get more. The effort required to accelerate my heart rate is more intense. That's why, when I have the impression I'm running my hardest, my heart is still, according to my trusty smartwatch, beating below average, and I have to work harder, train harder, push harder. So sometimes I'm an unforgiving and, frankly, insufferable person to be next to. That may explain why I love running so much. For this undeserved biological advantage, which means that even under great strain my heart remains in "energy saving" mode and therefore, counting the number of beats per second, can last longer before pooping out.

Before my doctor's visit I was so worried about firming up my muscles and ligaments that I hadn't realized that it isn't your calves that get the biggest workout when you run. It's your heart. I'm not sure whether I should be happy about my diagnosis, though I find something poetic about the anomaly—and ultimately, given my slow, intense approach to everything, it suits me. I just hope it doesn't bode ill for the marathon in Athens I'm so determined to run. The word bradycardia shares a root with the Italian word for sloth (brad-ipo), that unfortunate animal not known for its velocity, whose name, the opposite of Achilles' epithet, swift-footed, is in fact derived from bradys *(slow) and* pous *(foot).*

In the *Spartan Constitution*, Xenophon writes, "Lycurgus appeared convinced of one thing: that bearing children was the first and most noble function of freeborn women. Therefore, he instituted physical education for both the female and male sex. In addition to strength and speed competitions for men, he created competitions for women, believing that a child born to a strong father and strong mother would himself be strong."

2,500 years later, running was my feminist training grounds—and my battlefield.

I finally understood Simone de Beauvoir not by reading *The Second Sex* at the Café de Flore but by clocking miles along the Seine. And I felt neither anger nor the urge to revolt, but instead a deep compassion for all women, a kind of vague melancholy which hardened in me and has never gone away.

Of course, I didn't have to run to realize that I was born a woman, or rather, a human being of the female sex. And obviously there's no need for this book to attest to the many times, as a woman, people questioned my credibility and suitability, especially in the academic and cultural circles that I've always belonged to. For women to climb the ranks and receive equal treatment, it isn't enough for us to finish those twenty-six reserved for men; our marathon, to borrow a well-worn running metaphor, is a few dozen miles longer, and all unforgivingly uphill.

Before running, the conflicts I faced because I am a woman always arose from without, from men and a lack of respect I was shown along the way: an opportunity denied, a status unacknowledged, verbal abuse. Offenses that hurt, some of them deeply, but (fortunately) they couldn't breach my overall vision of womanhood and (unfortunately) never raised my consciousness or led me to fight back.

But a few months after I started to run, my being a woman became a source of bitter tension, and I was despondent for a while. For the first time in my life, the conflict didn't come from without—from, say, somebody on the street whistling at me as I ran by, a phenomenon that didn't happen daily but every few minutes when I was living in Rome.

No, the war was declared by me, in me.

I don't know whether femininity is really "secreted by the ovaries," as Simone de Beauvoir wonders aloud. I read her work—hardly what you'd call a guide to running—a lot while I was agonizing over whether to write this book and frequently driving myself to give it up. It was a decision I retracted at least a couple times.

Whatever my position on feminism is, I have, and have had since birth, two ovaries. And when you play sports, being equipped with two ovaries is often aggravating and always a burden. From general aches and pains to menstrual cycles to hormonal imbalances that painfully change the shape of your breasts, being a woman in an athletic competition and during the extended period needed to train for one can hardly be called a biological advantage.

Science still can't (or doesn't want to) tell us much about it. Performance apparel helps, though not much. Little can be done about it, that's just the way the female body works, and medicine can't change it—and why should it?

I once read somewhere that "a woman is a man who can run a marathon bleeding from start to finish." I appreciate the brevity and sting of that phrase, and I try to remember it during especially dizzying workouts.

Since I've been working on this book and training for my marathon in Athens, I often cross paths with other women on my morning runs. I can't help but wonder how they're feeling. If they, too, working their leg muscles as hard as they can, feel a kind of dead weight in their wombs, just below their belly buttons, or in some other part of themselves. In their souls, say. I often imagine stopping them to ask, but I'm too ashamed.

Men seem so carefree, so untroubled when they run that it never occurs to me to ask how they feel. But with women I feel a kind of tacit solidarity, a shared biology, a sense of goodwill and compassion. When I see women runners who are in much better shape than I am, I'm never envious, I never suffer an attack of jealousy. It must be on account of our common datum—our uterus—and the toil of carrying it with us on our runs that I have developed a deep sense of sisterhood with all the women I encounter, beginning with the Spartan women Xenophon describes, and the feeling doesn't fade when I remove my running shoes.

For that matter, in Italian the word for running (*corsa*), from the Latin *cursus*, past participle of the verb *correre* (to run), is a feminine noun. As is the word *resistenza* (persistence, endurance, resistance).

* * *

Obviously, women weren't allowed to participate in the ancient Olympics. Neither as participants (please!) nor as spectators. Breaking the law was punishable by death. The historian Pausanias describes how women caught attending the games were thrown from Mount Typaion, a mountain located on the road to Olympia.

There was, however, a sport reserved for members of the female sex at Olympia. It was called the Heraia, or Heraean Games, in honor of the goddess Hera, and was therefore religious in nature. It had nothing of the Olympics' secular majesty, it wasn't a celebration of human potential. Legend has it that these women's games were founded by Hippodamia, the daughter of Oenomaus, the king of Pisa (the Greek city, not its more famous Tuscan counterpart), to show gratitude to the goddess for her happy marriage to Pelops. The first winner was Chloris, the only surviving daughter of Niobe.

Though historians argue that the establishment of the Heraean Games was politically motivated, a ploy to ease tensions between Pisa and its rival Elis, they soon became known throughout Greece and were organized to take place the same year as the all-male Olympic Games by a committee of sixteen elderly women chosen to weave a votive robe for Hera. Competitors were split into three categories: girls, young ladies, and adults. The competition consisted of a single footrace, barely over 160 meters long, far shorter than the men's race. The women competed in chitons, extremely short tunics that exposed the right shoulder down to the breast, and wore their hair down. Plato himself observed that the uniform was indecent, hardly suitable for competitive sports. Winners received a portion of a cow sacrificed to Hera and an olive crown, as can be seen in a first century BC statue of an athlete by the sculptor Pasiteles now housed in the Vatican Museums, striking for its beauty and eroticism.

Whereas the Heraean Games can be seen as a rite of passage from adolescence to adulthood rather than a healthy competition among women, another female initiation race in ancient Greece boggles the mind. In Brauron, a town roughly twelve miles from Athens, runners were chased by a bear! Every four years a solemn procession accompanied these girls from the capital to the sacred site of Brauron, where they would live together for a time. They were called *arktoi*, or she-bears, in honor of the goddess Artemis, whose sacred animal was the bear. Dressed in crocus yellow tunics, a color that the Greeks associated with menstrual blood, the girls performed rituals and sacrifices before their final challenge: to flee from a bear that had been baited. Those who safely reached the finish line were, so it was believed, purified of their wild, primordial femininity and ready to take husbands, not to mention hang up their spurs (or running shoes) for good.

A husband rather than a trophy or glory was also the reward at the end of the most famous race in classical mythology, that of the beautiful Atalanta, whose story begins in violence simply because she was born a woman. Abandoned in the woods by a father who'd wanted a son and not some snotty girl, Atalanta was raised by a small group of hunters and a bear given to her by Artemis. As an adult, she became a fierce warrior who famously killed the Caledonian boar, among others, and was known throughout Greece for her great speed. Yet her extraordinary prowess was overlooked, once again, because of her sex. Apollonius of Rhodes recounts how Jason, the leader of the Argonauts, left her behind, refusing to take a woman on his travels to Colchis—something he'd soon regret. Her father had regrets, too. When he got word that the little girl he'd given up had become famous, he promptly demanded his daughter marry so that he could profit from her fame. Described as a sensual woman who took pride in being unmarried, Atalanta devised a scheme to avoid the fate predicted for her by an oracle, who told her that were she ever to marry, she'd lose her ability to run. Confident her legs couldn't be bested, she told her father that she'd only marry a man if he could beat her in a race. Any man who lost would be executed. One after another, her suitors failed to overtake her. Then came Melanion, who, following the advice of Aphrodite, dropped three golden apples at her feet during the race, forcing her to stop and retrieve them, and thus lose precious time. There's no account of the fortunes of Atalanta after the two were married, and in Greece people no longer spoke of this first mythic runner's races.

While other, religious-inflected women's sports were held throughout Greece, including the Dionysia in honor of Dionysus, women were eventually allowed to participate in the Olympics for one reason only: to finance chariot races. Which is to say that women were permitted to lend economic support to one of the costliest and most elite of ancient sports, but they could not participate in them. The so-called auriga who drove the chariot had to be male. Plutarch mentions Cynisca, a wealthy Spartan princess capable of financing her own team. Cynisca was the first woman to officially participate in the Olympics, in 336 BC, as an owner and racehorse trainer who earned her laurels when her team won a four-horse chariot race called the *te-thrippon*. According to sources, Cynisca was forty years old and unmarried when her team joined the race. Word of her exceptional feat spread throughout Greece, and two statues of her were placed in the temple of Olympus.

But it was not until the first century AD, when Greece was already under Roman control, and just before Philostratus put together his treatise on sports, that women participated in sports irrespective of religion. Sources attest to three unbeatable female runners, Tryphosa, Hedea, and Dionysia, who were honored with statues and high honors.

In Rome, women athletes were first permitted to participate in public games in 186 BC by order of the consul Marcus Fulvius Nobiliore, after a vote during the Aetolian War. Thereafter female sports enjoyed a healthy tradition. Especially when it came to running. In 86 AD Emperor Domitian established a woman's footrace as part of the Certamen Capitolino Iovi, and in the following century a woman won a race to honor Augustus's wife Livia. And, though gladiator games aren't really the same as sports events, not a few female gladiators, mostly slaves and peasants, lost their lives in the circus. A bas-relief recovered from Halicarnassus and dating to sometime between the first and second century AD depicts two female fighters—naked, again—squaring off in the cavea armed with shields and swords.

With the arrival of Christianity, all sports were believed to be a dangerous relic of paganism and outlawed. Women would have to wait almost two thousand years, until the Olympic Games in Paris, in 1900, before entering the Olympics stadium again.

In fact, at the first modern Olympiad organized in Athens in 1896 by Baron Pierre de Coubertin, female athletes were prohibited from competing and relegated to the sidelines to cheer. But one athlete—yet again a Greek, yet again a long-distance runner—defied this outrage. Stamata Revithi, a thirty-year-old mother of two, tried to sign-up for a race under the pseudonym Melpomene, the muse of tragedy. Her application rejected, she decided to run the Marathon in Athens anyway, alone, on April 11, 1896. She was stopped before she could reach the finish at the Panathenaic Stadium, but if those twenty-five miles can officially be run by everyone, even me, it's thanks to her and to all the women of the past who never stopped running, on or off the tracks already trod by men.

* * *

Some argue that athletes entered Olympic competitions completely naked because during the summer Greeks wanted to test their ability to endure the blazing sun. Be that as it may, the Greeks themselves say that the practice originated when Pherenice of Rhodes, daughter of the boxer Diagoras, had such a powerful character that she was at first mistaken for a man. She was thereby able to enter the Olympic stadium, hiding [disguising her sex] under a cloak, and train her son, Pisidorus. The boy was also a boxer, with strong hands for the sport, and had nothing to envy his famous grandfather. Though Pherenice's deception was uncovered, people were reluctant to execute her, for her family was full of Olympic winners. Though it was decided to spare her life, a law was passed obligating gymnasts to strip naked and pass a doctor's inspection.

As Philostratus' account shows, women have been forced to hide their womanhood since antiquity, disguising themselves as men so that they'll be taken seriously in running shoes.

Pherenice—according to other sources the brave *boxeuse* was known as Callipatera—was the first woman in history to compete against men. The last, we hope, was the legendary Kathrine Switzer, who in 1967 became the first woman to run an all-male marathon, in Boston, by registering under her initials, K.V. Switzer. She received bib number 261 because she'd been mistaken for a man.

Born to American parents in Germany in 1947, as a teenager Kathrine ran with men's sports teams because there were no university teams for women. At the time, the Olympic Committee barred women from running over eight hundred meters based on nothing but cheap prejudice, the absurd idea that if you were a woman who actively engaged in sports you would, as Switzer put it, "get big legs, grow a moustache and hair on your chest, and your uterus was going to fall out."

On April 19, 1967, the day of the race, Switzer appeared on the starting line defiantly wearing makeup and red lipstick. By her side, in a show of solidarity, were her coach and her boyfriend, a nationally ranked hammer thrower. At mile six, one of the race's organizers peremptorily ordered her to stop and the director literally leapt at her and tried to rip her bib off. "Get the hell out of my race," he screamed. The image has gone down in the history of sports and the feminist movement.

Apparently, Switzer told her coach: "I'm going to finish this race on my hands and knees if I have to. Because if I don't finish this race, nobody's going to believe women can do it." At the end of the marathon, she was rewarded for her bravery by being officially disqualified and suspended from the American Athletics Federation, which was deter-mined to bar women from long-distance running.

Ever since that April day in Boston, Kathrine Switzer hasn't once given up her fight to enshrine gender equal-ity in sports. In 1972, she finished a second marathon in Boston and in 1974 she won the New York marathon with an amazing time of three hours, seven minutes, and twen-ty-nine seconds. Then finally, in 1984, the first Women's Marathon took place at the Olympics in Los Angeles. On April 17, 2017, exactly half a century after her first historic run, seventy-year-old Kathrine Switzer ran her ninth mar-athon in Boston. Pinned to her chest was the number 261, the same she'd worn in 1967.

This must be what the Greeks call *kleos*, the glory that drove Homer's heroes to risk their lives on the battlefield, the fame that would grant them immortality, something to be handed down from father to son. Only in the case of Kathrine Switzer that immortal heroism gets passed down from mother to daughter.

* * *

From disguised female bodies to stripped, exposed, and sexualized bodies.

In Athens, the statesman Solon passed a law requiring all youth, except slaves, to engage in athletic activities. Apparently by youth Solon meant boys, seeing as women were denied access to gyms. Still, if footraces were the domain of men in most *poleis*, Sparta was, yet again, the exception. Not only were athletics widely endorsed for the education of young women to ensure they give birth to strong and healthy children, but there was also an exclusively female event called *endromis*, which consisted of racing, fighting, jumping, shot put, and the javelin throw. *Endromis* came with a strange twist, described by Plutarch: the women had to compete in public naked.

More than two thousand years later, the fact that most (read: nearly all) of the extant literature about the art of running is written by men never troubled me much, at least not at first. Maybe that's because I'm an optimist, or a naïf, when it comes to interpreting the world, or maybe my cowardice mentioned at the start of this book is to blame. I think it's the latter, which has always kept me from seriously trying to change things, entrusting that work to the spirit of the times, a concept as generic as it is vague.

Before I took up running, Kathrine Switzer's heroic acts hadn't inspired me much. Moved me, yes, but feeling broadly moved by the triumphs of a handful of independent men and women may be the toxin that keeps the rest of us from being actively committed. I was aware that it was thanks to Switzer that I could sign up for any race in the world I wanted to, from the hundred-meter dash to a hundred-mile ultratrail through the forest. Of course I warmly acknowledged my debt to her, just as I acknowledge my debt to the suffragettes who fought to ensure my right to vote, but that was about it, and it never rose above the level of superficial esteem.

Instead, the jogging suits targeted toward women shoppers by every sporting goods brand, many of them pastels that border on the pornographic, not only never shocked me, but, for a time, made me proud of my unconscious sexualization.

Completely ignorant of feminism, and surely many

other things, I never realized, running in form-fitting pink nylon—one of the trendiest colors in gyms and nurseries—that parading around like that was not a personal choice but the only option afforded me by fashion companies for amateur women runners who are forced unawares to finance an industry that wants them to be seen as sensual, like dolls, even when they're sweating and hobbling under the sun, by men, who are outfitted with minimalist gravity, like champion athletes (even when they're not).

Nothing new under the sun of subliminal—because difficult to decipher—misogyny. In one of the rare works of art depicting ancient female athletes, women are shown wearing skimpy bathing suits. The famous fourth-century mosaic in the Sala delle Palestrite, a room in the Villa Romana del Casale, just outside Piazza Armerina, Sicily, looks more like a beauty contest than an aerobic session. Nine beautiful athletes, in dazzling and extraordinarily modern shape, pass around a ball, throw a discus, and lift weights, all while striking sexy and provocative poses. We know nothing about these women, neither their sport of choice nor what medals they may have won. All we know is that they're wearing what is regarded as the first bikini in the history of art.

The latest position to be taken on the world stage occurred when the German women's gymnastics team showed up at the Tokyo Olympics wearing full body suits—a fashion choice usually made for religious reasons—rather than the dainty, sequined leotards that made the sport famous. "We wanted to show that every woman, everybody, should decide what to wear," explained champion Elisabeth Seitz, demanding the respect already due the beach volleyball players: to be recognized for their athletic achievement rather than for the morsels of skin offered up for public consumption.

In ancient times, Spartan men would attend sports events and shamelessly evaluate the naked bodies of women athletes to choose their future wives, as if it were a market of female flesh. And to this day there are many women's sports that men claim to follow on TV for the pure pleasure of admiring two firm buttocks filling out a pair of shorts.

Personally, I've always been fond of seduction, making ample use of my body as well as my mind. Yet what I didn't know before feeling literally indecent while running was the same thing Plato noted when he beheld the spectacle of half-naked women athletes: that our bodies are often sexualized a priori, without our even realizing it. We look sexy not by choice but because someone has made the decision for us, and this is so ingrained in us that we struggle to be aware of it. Whereas even the most educated and evolved men enjoy the spectacle offered up to them by the ideological system into which we are all born.

On the sidewalks of Paris and the dusty fields of Sparta, the female body engaged in physical activity isn't seen for what it is—a combination of muscles and tendons, of labor and persistence, no different from that of a man's or an animal's in the act of exerting itself—but rather as a kind of show to entertain, turn on, arouse curiosity, invite disapproval, and pass erotic or aesthetic judgment on.

This realization troubled me greatly.

No, I didn't stop wearing shorts or purchasing clothes

from major sporting goods brands once I'd rooted out the hypocrisy. But I did become conscious of it. Now I'm the one commanding the seduction. I decide when to seduce, and how. And I've never felt so free—free to run, and free to be sexy.

I do it on behalf of the beautiful girls in the Sicilian mosaic, and for all the other women in the history of sports.

* * *

But the real clash between my being a woman, writer, and amateur runner began when for the first time I felt the desire to be a mother.

About this subject, our Philostratus dares to write:

> The Spartan Lycurgus had already anticipated something even more respectable: to ensure the Spartans had combat-ready athletes, he decreed that women should be trained and free to run in public so that by virtue of their training they would bear hardy progeny. This way, after marriage, women wouldn't complain about carrying water or grinding grain, because they'd have grown accustomed to exercise. And if their husbands were young and athletic, women would have even better progeny, for their children would be slender, strong, and perfectly healthy. By observing these rules of marriage, the Spartans prevailed in battle.

I can't get behind forms of historical relativism that would dismiss the Greeks as misogynists and sexists and toss them and their texts onto the burn pile. I'm firmly convinced that the words "cancel" and "culture" can't appear in the same sentence without the risk of the one nullifying the other, and making things even worse. But neither can I deny that the words of Philostratus, who like nearly all ancient authors was a coddled and pampered scion of his time, make me shudder, out of irritation more than shock.

When I was a girl, I struggled to understand why Simone de Beauvoir would claim the freedom to be a writer and not a mother, endorsing the idea that the two are incompatible.

When I was a woman, this dilemma detonated in my hands one day, as if I'd stumbled onto a mine in the park. Further complicating matters was a third prospect, which I had been naively nurturing and which gravely exacerbated the situation: the wish to be a writer and mother *and* run a marathon.

I don't feel like expressing an opinion on the connection between maternity and writing just this moment—though somewhere deep inside me I have the nagging suspicion that Beauvoir was right and that everything that I've written is a prelude to failure, both personal and literary—but I know for certain that it is physically, biologically impossible to train for a marathon when you're pregnant or planning a pregnancy.

I have no doubt that, out in the world, there are many exceptions to this, and that there exist pregnant women who can run two hundred miles a month. Still, whatever Lycurgus said in Sparta, planning to run a marathon while also planning to get pregnant is strongly discouraged by almost all licensed doctors. According to science, the intense physical strain of running long distances appears to affect a woman's hormonal balance and, therefore, the (at least biological side of her) femininity secreted from her ovaries.

It was dispiriting for me to discover all that one day, a bit randomly on the internet—there's no point waiting for special "running while pregnant" stories to appear in sports magazines; paradoxically, it is the classics that tackle the subject, however wrongheadedly.

It was the first, indelible, searing time in my life that I was forced to scrap a plan that I believed in just because I was born a woman—and there was nothing at all I could do about it.

The biology didn't upset me. I'd long known that a good part of me is the result of a dance of hormones which enables me to create life once a month, and I have always been proud of that fact.

What wounded me deeply was the knowledge that one choice precluded another. It was either marathon or maternity. Either/or.

Sure, I could have planned accordingly and pursued both projects at different points in time, but that wouldn't have changed anything. Because I was a woman I had to throw my hands up and choose. To learn to work hard and not, as Philostratus says, "complain," if I hoped to bear hale and hearty children.

In this Beauvoir was right, at least as concerns the conflict between maternity and running.

And who knows how many conflicts, how many either/ors and this or thats are out there waiting to slap us women in the face.

The thought haunted me for a long time.

Not because for once in my life I had to give up my desire to control events and stop planning. But because of the unfair logic of the situation: were I born a man, this ordinary change of plans in my life wouldn't exist.

Not to mention the leisurely idea that men have of

conception. A man can spend nine months lovingly clasping the hand of his pregnant partner, but the pregnancy itself—the change, the struggle, the life—do not pass directly through his body. It is a fact that he can't feel these things.

He can imagine them, sure. He can summon all the empathy in the world. But he can't physically feel them with his five senses. Indeed, he's cut out. If he wants, he can run a marathon a week. Nothing that he decides to do to his body, good or bad, influences the health of his baby.

I don't know how Spartan women put up with it. Personally, I never felt the divide to be so clear-cut, distinct, stagnant.

Strangely, I never missed my partner so much as those days spent weighing the need to choose between running a marathon and fulfilling my desire to be a mother, even though he was right there by my side. I wanted to ask him for help, but I couldn't. Biologically, physically, he could neither run for me nor carry my baby. He could understand, and he did the best he could, but he couldn't feel what I felt. The mutual understanding rooted in experience that had always bound us together was denied us a priori.

They say that we're never so alone as when we run. But I felt alone before it ever crossed my mind to run.

In the end, I decided to try to hold all three things together: running, writing, womanhood. Well aware of my limitations.

If my final time turns out to be second rate—and surely it will, at the end of the marathon my performance won't be worth remembering, and it's highly likely this book will meet the same fate—at least I'll be able to say that I set my own limits and didn't have them handed down to me by some man named Lycurgus.

J uly has put in its first appearance, the days are growing shorter, though no one has caught on yet. In the
past weeks Paris has become so gray and wet it's like
Brittany, only landlocked and dark. My partner has gone to
the south, and I find there's no better cure for missing him
than a run.

It's incredible, sometimes heartwarmingly innocent, how
much running has become the quick answer to every incident
in my life, great or small. Has the day been exhausting? I
think I'll go out for a run then. Important meeting tomorrow? Nothing like a quick jog to steady the nerves. Are you
so happy you can't contain it? A couple miles on the street
and I'll relish it even more. Feeling sad, angry, confused,
sluggish, frustrated? In a half hour you and your negative
feelings will have called a ceasefire and begun the peace process. For the last three years, no matter what's going on in
my life, my answer to everything is always: "I'm going for a
run." It's my problem-solving go-to—the only one that does
the trick.

Today is Sunday and by now running has become my favorite weekend pastime, the supreme luxury, fulfilling not only
because it's free time but because I desire to do something
with it as honorable as taking a run, as waking up early and

eluding the vices of body and soul. I find it so gratifying that last night, a Saturday in Montmartre in the middle of summer, I went to bed at ten already dreaming of how I would get up in the morning and run one of my favorite routes. Had someone ever told me that running, and not cocktails or dinner parties or after-dinner parties, would become my recreation of choice, I'd have either burst out laughing or become seriously concerned about my mental health.

Nine miles at a relaxed clip, a base run, a slow and steady pace, a moderate effort that leaves a runner with enough breath in their lungs to speak (if, unlike me, you've ever had something interesting to say on a run) and can be maintained for long distances without having a meltdown. This is my long weekly run, which enables me to cool down yet make the most of my shorter, more intense workouts during the week. It's my favorite, because I don't start running well until I've crossed the three-mile threshold. More importantly, it gives me the chance to get in the famous flow that, at least for me, never materializes if I haven't fully warmed up or gotten over the exertion of starting my run. Whatever others say, compared to walking, running is still difficult and unnatural.

This weekend I've chosen the Parc de la Villette, the least Parisian of Paris' parks and to my surprise the one I like best, so much so that I begin to miss it when I've been away from it for long. In the morning, especially on weekends, this very urban and anti-Haussmann green space in the XIX arrondissement morphs into Paris' running mecca. We all come here to run: men, women, boys, girls, sometimes even children. Some run with their dogs, others wear trail gear. There are neighborhood firemen and running teams, the young and the not-so-young. At ten sharp, as if by tacit agreement, we gather in front of the large silver ball (that houses a movie theater) opened in the 1980s by Francois Mitterrand, pleased to toil and sweat and run for miles, skirting bottles of beer from the night before.

Clichéd, even a little pathetic, as it may sound, one reason I'm happy to run at the Villette on weekends is this sense of community. I've always had a hard time feeling like I belong to something. Prior to Paris, I was disloyal to every city I lived in. I've never been part of a team, group, fraternity, or political party. In the world of soccer fandom, my allegiance wavered from this team to that. But when I come here to run, I feel part of a diverse community of runners, even if I know nothing about my companions in the sport, not what they do or where they're from. I don't even know their names! I do know that we share something deeper than a few personal details. I know that these men and women outfitted in technical apparel and futuristic shoes can relate to what I'm feeling when I run. They don't need to imagine it. They feel it. Sometimes I think that it would be incredibly easy for us to become friends and maybe share a stretch of this road of life together because, thanks to this endeavor we have in common, running, we already know one another and share more things, more values, than with any other stranger happily met about whom we know nothing.

They say the same happens among motorcyclists: When they meet on the street, they greet one another, signaling that they belong to an exclusive community, separate from all the drivers shut inside their steel boxes. I'm not so insane as to greet every runner I meet in the morning, not yet at least, but we do share a glance, almost always one of satisfaction and pride. That, yes, happens often.

If I run, or continue to run, rather, it's thanks to all the runners with whom I've crossed paths in the morning, on short runs and long. Watching perfect strangers persevere and never quit keeps me from quitting. Coming across a person intently running in the rain makes me feel less alone, less insane. Passing someone slower than me reminds me of the compassion that I was unable to concede to myself when I was starting out. And being passed by someone in better shape has motivated me to give my legs an even harder workout.

In short, should I ever reach the end of the Athens Marathon, it'll be thanks to all the runners who have inspired me simply by running beside me.

Today's run was long, but positive. I was pleased, as I am whenever I run here. My feelings of nostalgia didn't completely vanish, but they did subside a little. Now I can go home satisfied, ready to respond to the next thorn in my side: Thanks, but I'm going for a run.

VI
Born to Run

I still don't know whether running is a natural phenomenon.

I'm not sure that without a strong psychological incentive—my fear of aging, hence my terror of dying—I would continue to run regularly just because some of my cells naturally demanded I run. On the contrary, I seriously doubt it.

More than once on my route I have wondered whether we ought to consider running a need of the body or an imposition, however pleasant, of the mind; whether our legs naturally desire to run to overcome the unnatural sedentary position in which we're forced to spend a large part of our days, or whether our brain is urging our feet to continue to make an effort that goes against their nature.

I'm not talking about the decision to hit the couch rather than take a run after a long day at the office. I'm not talking about tenacity and the desire to see a marathon through, either. What I want to know is where this sudden desire to run, which has transformed Western society into a kind of giant sports team that makes no distinction between class or ability, comes from. Is it all in our heads? A slew of psychoanalytic impulses that Freud could describe better than I, which can be summed up in the phrase "running makes me feel good," one as simple as it is banal? Or is it a natural need of the body, like eating, drinking, and sleeping?

On a broader political and sociological level, I'm interested to know whether our current way of looking at running is really a reflection of its being the most democratic of sports, as runners, chuffed after a few laps around the neighborhood and thinking they're the Che Guevaras of the increasingly sophisticated and expensive sports world, insist it is, or whether it is just the result of an ideology that demands women and men be better looking, younger, healthier, and thinner for longer, which in actuality makes us slaves to the sport, rather than pioneers.

Are we all naturally made for running or is the ultimate goal of our organisms peace and quiet, a state of rest without external stimuli? Are our legs meant to travel roads less taken or stand still and safely, soberly take in the view?

"Tramps like us, baby, we were born to run," sings Bruce Springsteen. In third-century Greece, Philostratus agreed. Sports are innate to man. Running, wrestling, and boxing came into being as soon as the first human being appeared in the world. The reason they were created can be traced to the birth of man: "Just as iron and copper gave rise to the blacksmith's art, just as the bounty of the earth gave rise to farming and the sea accounts for sailing, gymnastics is a natural and intimate extension of being human."

The philosopher doesn't stop there. He goes on to say the first athlete in history was Prometheus, he who spawned human civilization by stealing Zeus's fire and giving it to man. Prometheus's coach, apparently, was none other than Hermes, architect of the first gym, who passed down his knowledge to the subversive Titan. And the first men on

Earth, who were still delicately built and weak, trained in the mud under the guidance of Prometheus, who was convinced that sports would ready their limbs for whatever life threw at them.

It makes complete sense. Ever since the first day of creation (if you're a believer) or since the latest stage of evolution (if you're a skeptic), sports have been regarded as an extraordinary triumph of civilization. The invention of gymnastics represents our transcendence from a primitive, animal state, which compelled hunter to chase prey and weak to escape strong. In a way, it's a major democratic achievement, because thanks to working out everyone can escape an enemy or procure food and no longer needs to be protected, or avoid being crushed, by the burliest member of the pack. Whatever the case, scientists say that our ability to run, and not our erect posture, was the real evolutionary leap that thousands of years ago led to our transformation from Australopithecus to Homo habilis, paving the way, or the route, for our species.

Sports were, then, a means for mankind to gain freedom and make progress, to liberate itself from its primitive and unevolved state, from a savage society ruled by the tyranny of the strong and the submission of the weak, starting with that quintessential civilizing hero, Prometheus. After all, running as a means to gain freedom, a triumphal march, is one of the most well-worn metaphors in the history of film, beginning with *The Shawshank Redemption*, a film based on a short story by Stephen King. When have we ever not seen a prisoner set off running, elated, once they've broken their chains?

Still, I'm not completely convinced that more muscles for everybody equals more freedom for everybody. At least not today. I often feel that for many people, including my-self, sports has become not a door flung open but a cage we willingly enter. Maybe it's the slightly downhearted words and fatalist tones that runners preparing for a race use to talk about their training, like "I've got a long session today" or "tomorrow I have to do intervals," where what is audible isn't enthusiasm but the kind of sigh of defeat you expect to hear at the back of the line at the post office. Maybe it's the relentless-to-the-point-of-stalking appeals that institutions and the media make, urging us to exercise in order to stay healthy. Or maybe it's just because running means suffer-ing, often a lot, whereas satisfying other natural needs, like eating, sleeping, and having sex, gives us satisfaction and pleasure.

Whatever the reason, on mornings when I'm stopped at a traffic light on the Seine and elbow-to-elbow with runners lined up single-file as they wait for the light to turn green, weary and sweat-soaked in our hi-tech ap-parel, I have the impression that we're all following some perverse order or that by running we're doing penance, so that afterward we can live out the normal course of a day trouble-free.

Unlike the initial evolutionary leap, that spurt of free-dom and progress, in the last thirty or forty years our sports madness hasn't liberated Western society (from what ex-actly?) but rather, it seems, suppressed and enslaved it.

To play with the tragedies of Aeschylus, the road back-ward from *Prometheus Unbound* to *Prometheus Bound* is an instant. Or maybe I'm being a pessimist because I can't stand to run anymore.

* * *

I have a body.

It's such a simple and obvious statement that it seems dumb to write it down, subject and predicate. Yet I swear that before running I wasn't aware I had a body. I didn't even know I had thoughts—I mean *concrete, tangible thoughts*—but running has taught me so many things that I often wonder what I knew about myself before I picked it up.

No other activity that I've practiced in my life has brought me so close to my physical consciousness: not traveling or eating or making love. Writing least of all. Writing means forgetting all about your body for months and years.

What I mean is that, like everyone else, I've been totally aware of having two legs, two arms, two hands, etc., ever since, I think, I opened my eyes and began to catalog the appearance of human beings to distinguish them from cats, plants, and mosquitoes. Or maybe I was already aware of it when I was taking the measurement of things in my mother's belly.

I knew it, but I didn't feel it. My outrageously robust body was never really a cause for concern, nor was it fodder for half-baked philosophies. That it would always do whatever I wanted it to—including things I shouldn't do—seemed to me a given, something that should come as no surprise, part of the natural order of things, like the sun that shines, the sky above our heads, the smell of sunscreen in the summer.

And, as an heir to Western culture with Judeo-Christian roots I never took much interest (read: no interest at all) in the bustle of cells that I'm made of, unless I was studying them in a biology textbook, and it was almost vulgar—frivolous, surely—to devote time to the mechanics of the body at the expense of training my neurons.

I told myself that if two thousand years ago the West regarded the body as nothing but a container, the Tupperware of the soul, then I might as well put all my energy into the latter. I have a vague recollection of giving up swimming lessons just before entering *liceo classico* and not shedding a tear about it. On the contrary, I was happy to sacrifice a few hours of sports at the altar of Greek and Latin. Honestly, I couldn't find time in the afternoon for anything besides homework and test prep.

When I started to run it was like a window had been opened onto the matter I'm made of, the matter we're all made of. Suddenly, for the first time, I could no longer expect my legs, heart, and miserable lungs to do my bidding. For a pitifully long time they didn't.

All at once, my body came into existence. There it was, begging me for all sorts of things: to eat, to rest, to train, and to be shown respect. It intimated to me who I am and where I come from. It held me in its grip and made me listen.

For the first time my body made itself felt and had the floor; I could hear its voice. Always caught up in my thoughts, I was now being forced to ask what, besides four friendly neurons, I really was. It was as if someone was happily adjusting the lens through which I was accustomed to looking at the world and which had long been trained on the outside world for me to catalog, understand, and deconstruct. When I ran, the focus abruptly shifted to my inner being, to the matter I'm made of.

When I was a girl, Homer, Plato, Aeschylus, and all

the other ancient Greeks taught me that I had a head and ought to use it. Now that I am an adult, a pair of running shoes has shown me that I have a body and that something more, something beyond its being the seat of the mind, can be done with it.

As for its being natural, I'm not sure what to say. But I know that ancient Greek and running have shown me that any talent can and must be cultivated in order to feel well and, in the end, derive a shred of good from it.

There comes a time in life when whatever talent you've been given is no longer enough and the hope that you can continue to profit from a handful of such gifts without working at them turns out to be ridiculous. If, that is, you were lucky enough to discover what they are in the first place.

I don't know if it's the clearest sign of growing old, but at a certain point, without warning, the reserves of talent that we once greedily drew on begin to run low. It's terrifying to find they're gone, in short supply, insufficient. Replenishing them through training and dedication, physical or intellectual, is hard but necessary work.

It's hard to see running long distances, absent clear and present dangers, as something our species does instinctively. I have no doubt that a leopard, spotting us scurrying down the concrete wearing headphones and neon leggings, would think we're crazy. It's equally hard to think that spending six hours a day bent over a Greek dictionary written in print so fine it may have been scrawled by a scribe or translating tragedies about infanticide and incest is the most natural way to spend your adolescence.

Just as I have never encountered a high school student

overjoyed at the prospect of wading through a Latin text-book, I've never heard a runner sing the praises of running while running. Look at the sad faces, more contorted than Laocoön's, that everybody from the Sunday jogger to Usain Bolt makes when they run, not without a little embarrassment. Oddly, as soon as they've snatched up their diploma or torn off their sneakers, these same people praise the moral superiority of the humanities or the noble art of sports.

Natural or not, a paradox clearly exists. We're never happy while we're studying or running, but we are happy, very happy, once we've stopped.

As I write these words I can't say exactly how many students on this planet are studying the humanities. But I know for a fact that every year more than a billion pairs of running shoes are sold worldwide.

The demands of both are considerable, the dedication they require heroic. Personally, when I began to run and seriously feared suffocating to death or having a heart attack just a few minutes down the road, nothing gave me the strength to keep at it, the will to survive, like the memory of those five years spent translating ancient Greek at eight in the morning, an hour when nowadays I couldn't even tell you my name.

Running is one of those human activities that do not function until we're through with them: they please us most not when we plow ahead but once we've called it quits.

Like marriage, remarked one friend drily.

* * *

Socrates: I'd say it seems that a god has given men two arts, the one intellectual ("the art of the muses") and the other physical ("gymnastics"), which form the foundation of their education and knowledge. And not in the specific interest of the soul or body alone, but in the interest of both, so they can be in harmony, to balance their degree of tension and relaxation.

Not only Sparta and Athens, not only the former's strict system of discipline and obedience known as *agoghé*, nor the latter's *paideia*, that same, human-centered, well-balanced education that Socrates describes in Plato's *Republic*. Every civilization, in every age, has taken a position on the merits of physical exercise based on their own ideological system.

The term "physical education" was introduced in France in the mid-1700s by the physician Jacques Ballexserd, who wrote an important paper arguing that physical exercise was an essential part of childhood development. Soon after, the French Revolution helped spread physical education far and wide, because only a population that is strong and robust, rather than weak and starving, can aspire to complete emancipation. Apparently the revolution needed sharp minds and quick feet. In 1852 the first university dedicated to sports was founded: Paris's *école normale* of gymnastics, the École de Joinville (now the Institut National du Sport, de l'Expertise et de la Performance).

In Italy, physical education was first taught in the Kingdom of Sardinia with the passage of the Casati Law in 1859, under the umbrella term "gymnastics," and originally mandatory for male children only. In 1878, after the unification of Italy, the minister of Public Education Francesco De Sanctis transformed the discipline, renaming it "educational gymnastics" (later just "physical education") and allowing young women to participate. The course of study was designed by the office of public education and the war department (hence the mandate for males) in order to "renew the blood, rebuild the fiber, increase vitality," said De Sanctis. The curriculum remained unchanged for over a century, until 2010, when physical education was replaced by "motor and athletic sciences," a controversial term which was itself replaced by the original term, physical education, in nursery and elementary schools.

I belong to the unfortunate generation for whom PE class consisted of kicking a ball around the school's run-down jungle gym. Except for routine swimming lessons at the public pool when I was around eight, all I remember of those two hours a week devoted to sports was the racket my male classmates made (as soon as they'd left behind their books and notebooks, they seemed to morph into a pack of animals huddled around a sponge ball), and the smell of sweat that occasionally overpowered the smell of the cafeteria, and our white gym shoes (this was long before Italians adopted the English word "sneakers"), and the overall sense of liberation, as if it were a break from the slog of school, given the general impression that PE was not to be taken as seriously as other subjects.

During PE we also ran. I distinctly remember having to run laps around a courtyard that couldn't have been more than twenty yards, and the dramatic scenes of those who didn't want to run and would suddenly fake an illness, and the world-champion looks of agony on the faces of those who ran outside of school, too, and wanted everybody to know it. Once a year there were also cross-country races: mini ultra-trails through some suburban fields where they sent the star athletes. Obviously, I wasn't one of them.

For me, unlike the translations of Greek and Latin that still haunt my dreams, gym class wasn't all that traumatic. I don't hold a grudge against the brave teacher who let us blow off steam after we'd been stuck in our seats for hours and had to bear the burden of getting the ardent spirits and violent hormones of early adolescence under control. Yet I would never, ever say that gym class sparked my interest in running. I didn't reject it out of hand either. For a long time my takeaway from gym class was a superficial indifference to sports.

Murakami says the same and says it well: his sudden passion for running, which didn't surface until he was in his thirties, had nothing to do with taking PE in his youth, because at school you are forced to play sports, compelled by your teacher and the system, whereas as an adult you choose to play sports of your own free will.

"Pray for a sound mind in a sound body," writes Juvenal in *Satire X*, coining a now well-worn phrase. I'm not a sociologist, but the increasingly overweight bodies of adults and children, due to poor diets and a widespread and palpable anxiety that can be felt everywhere, as if we were experiencing a collective nervous breakdown, often raise doubts about the physical and psychological health of contemporary society.

When asked what motivates them, one reason that a large majority of runners most often cites is health. Whether to shed a few happy-hour pounds or to stretch their legs that have been captive under a desk, whether to relax after a stressful day of balancing work and family or to air some ideas in pursuit of new projects, health benefits are what distinguish amateur running, running with no specific goals, otherwise known as jogging or "footing" (a pseudo-anglicism that took hold in Europe at the beginning of the twentieth century), from running as a discipline that falls under the noble category of track and field.

To feel better, to stay (or get) in shape, to look after your cardiovascular and psychic health: these are excellent reasons to endure a six-mile run, but at the same time it means this kind of running is not a sport, because it is divorced from competition, from the drive to reach a finish line (unless that finish line is a number on the scale). Indeed, this salutary aspect places jogging outside the framework of physical education and makes it more like a child's game, an experience where children can shirk the rigid postures of their parents and explore their surroundings simply by letting their hair down, simply by letting themselves live.

When we run for pleasure and not to compete with others or come out victorious, we're not playing sports, we're playing like rascals, like Carlo Collodi's wooden boy Pinocchio who gets into all sorts of trouble as he dashes ahead.

In his book *Les jeux et les hommes* (Man, Play and Games), French sociologist and esteemed translator of Borges Roger Caillois analyzes human play and draws a distinction between games that emerge spontaneously, or *paideia* (from Greek *pais*, child), and games with clear rules, or *ludus*, from Latin, fun games, from which we get the word ludic. The latter is what we call sports.

When rules, time limits, codes of conduct and objectives are applied to taking a kick, or thwacking a ball with a racquet, or simply running, the game stops being an expression of childlike freedom and turns into an organized sport.

Games, it would seem, are natural—like children, baby

animals also discover the world by playing them—while sports aren't. Tied to a specific society or moment in history, the fortunes of sports vary from century to century and country to country. But all children, from the first to last, in every corner of the world, have felt the irrepressible urge to play games.

This makes the stories told by the many runners who cross Africa on foot all the more strange and moving. Seeing these Western runners hustling across the Sahara, local children, not understanding it is a race and mistaking it for the most natural and spontaneous of games, begin to run next to them.

* * *

Amateur, i.e., noncompetitive, running subverts the logical order of things that would have children's games give way to adult sports.

With competition out of the way, this passion for running returns to being the kind of play for the sake of play that we experience in childhood, the one purpose of which is to give us pleasure. There are no set rules in jogging: no one forces a runner to stick to a path or maintain a certain pace or reach a particular speed.

A runner can run a lot or a little, fast or slow, up or down, every day or once a month, however and whenever he feels like, and no one will ever chide him for it. You don't have to follow one route; there are as many routes as there are roads in the world. When I train, I alternate between three different routes depending on how much time I have and the view I want. The world could care less about how fast I run each, and that's how it should be.

If there are endless ways to run, technical requirements become insignificant. There are none, in fact. Not only is technical apparel not indispensable; for some people it's superfluous. Take the new trend, which blew up after the publication of Christopher McDougall's bestseller *Born to Run*, of running shoeless. According to these joggers, who proudly call themselves "barefoot runners," the practice reduces the risk of injury, enhances the strength of your feet and the flexibility of your tendons, and generally cuts down on the amount of effort it takes to run. There are also proponents of running naked, but that's another story.

If the jogs around the living room that became legendary during the recent pandemic are any indication, you don't need a road to a run, either. In China, a man ran over forty miles up and down his hallway!

It is thanks to this apparently limitless freedom of play that runners never tire of running, unlike children who, after a few minutes of fiddling with one toy, soon grow bored and demand another. And maybe it is thanks to this playfulness and total liberation that, in the last decade, running has attracted hundreds of new recruits every day. France alone has an estimated 13 million amateur runners, compared to a mere 300 thousand professional athletes registered with the country's national athletic federation.

You can run where you like, when you like, as you like. The one rule of jogging is that there are no rules! Once we've completed our own private "level one"—three miles in the neighborhood park, say, or a marathon in New York—another level awaits, kind of like a videogame that never seems to end. Our initial enjoyment of the game transforms into a pleasure in running longer, or faster, or running in a city instead of open country, from a first run in the rain to a first in the mountains, until our first marathon and beyond—along with a first defeat and, for the lucky few, a first victory.

Without this constant reinvention, which makes us feel like pioneers every time we lace up our running shoes, it'd be impossible to keep running for years and not grow bored and press on to the next sport.

This playful quality may be the best thing about running. How long or how brief we can keep our breath doesn't matter, nor does it matter when our calves beg for mercy: each session is unique because each has a unique goal. A runner rarely, if ever, puts on her running shoes and goes out into the street without having at least a rough idea of how many miles she intends to run before throwing in the towel. This way, every single race is a personal triumph or failure and can't be compared to other people's times. In fact, the one metric by which we can judge a run is the previous day's run.

Though a lot of time has passed since, out of hubris or madness, I embarked on this literary endeavor to run a marathon in order to write about how you train for one, I still remember clearly the first mile I ran without stopping. I'm prouder of it than I am of my (much) later twelve-mile run, because it was the first concrete proof, the first confirmation that I, too, could run, and I was this close to weeping and crying out, like Philippides, "We've won!"

Heraclitus writes in a fragment, "A lifetime is a child playing, playing checkers: to the child goes the kingdom." If amateur running is a game, then the road belongs to us runners. Running is our kingdom.

Just as running doesn't require rules, it doesn't require

special gear and equipment either; all it takes is a body and the drive to get moving.

This Franciscan simplicity would seem to make running *the* democratic sport, the only one for which an athlete doesn't need a special place to train (a field, an equipment room, a pool) or a set time of day (you can run in the middle of the night; there are plenty of insomniacs who run by the light of the moon) or a wallet thick enough to permit her to cross the threshold of a sporting goods store. Running doesn't discriminate by gender, class or geographic location. A sturdy physique is the one requirement, and if it's true that not everyone has a soul, we all possess a body. And the exceptional feats of paralympic athletes, which would make an ancient Greek hero proud, prove that you don't even need two legs to run.

Flawless though that logic may be, running recently taught me the opposite. I've never in my life been in a field as elitist and classist as running. The unequal distribution of talent is almost cruelly discriminatory and totally irreversible.

True, we can spend a lifetime trotting around our local park at a modest clip and no one would ever look down on us for our lack of athletic talent. If anything, the contrary is true, given the bizarre respect—deference almost—that runners typically command as they whiz by people who stick to strolling the streets. It's equally true that I could take twelve hours to finish the Athens Marathon without it affecting my pride, or the pride of those close to me, in the least bit.

It's not a question of performance, but possibility. We're all free to run, but the epithet given to Achilles in the *Iliad*, swift-footed, doesn't attach itself to a lot of people. Not many at all, actually. Almost none.

If the level of training is the same, the difference between a mediocre time and an excellent time is determined by a talent written somewhere in the DNA of the lucky winner of a divine sports lottery. And there's nothing that can change that, not a petition or a revolution, because this physical, biological inequity is permanently embedded in our muscles and blood. There are natural runners—athletes and heroes—and then there's the rest of us. Even if we trained all our lives, we'd never catch up to the footprints left in the dust by their swift feet.

It seems like no big deal, like a biological fact, but the discovery of this outmoded classism that divides runners into one of two categories—the born-to-run nobility and the shapeless mass of plebes who are born to do something else but who still strive to run—unsettled me. Not that I had hoped, at thirty years old and after a lifetime of torpor and alcohol, that a few jogs would turn me into an Olympic champion. What left me feeling not hurt but tamed, resigned, like a conquered population, was the absolute certainty that, even if I had started running when I was still in my diapers and never quit, I still would never have become a champion.

This obvious and unresolvable disparity between those who possess talent and those who will never possess it may be the most anti-modern side of running and of sports in general, because it strikes at the root of the contemporary idea that, with hard work and dedication, one can arrive wherever one wants and be whomever one chooses. The very idea of progress, the dogma of our day and age, is thrown into question, because, sure, we can always get better by training, but we can never surpass our physical limitations, our given share of talent.

Before I started running, I had never been told "no" so bluntly, brazenly, categorically. After being raised to believe that studying was the one way to reverse disadvantageous social or political conditions and with the almost Calvinist conviction that all my hard work would sooner or later pay off, as a runner I realized how unequally talent is distributed among human beings and how impossible it is to remedy.

Thanks to running I finally understood that genetics, or a god, had established a perimeter for me from the moment I was born, and within that perimeter I can, and must, strive to do better. Yet no matter what I do, whatever strategy I adopt or price I'm willing to pay, I'll never be able to break past it.

Two thousand years ago, Philostratus presented a portrait of the ideal runner that borders on discrimination against those of us who are not ideal:

> To run well, one first needs to know how to stand upright. For the body to be in perfect proportion, the legs must be in line with the shoulders, the chest smaller than average and able to keep the stomach in good health; the knees flexible, the legs straight, the arms a little longer than normal. The muscles must be harmoniously developed because excessive muscle growth can hamper, so to speak, speed.

The philosopher also described the ideal runner's temperament, which, following Hippocrates's taxonomy, ought to be "hot" and "humid."

In today's neurotic age of body acceptance and aesthetic

Nazism, the slim sculpted body is what's in fashion, and it has altered our perception of beauty, presenting fitness fanatics as a model to follow. But the inequality of running has nothing to do with aesthetics: ugly or beautiful, you're either born with talent or you aren't.

If statistics show that most runners darting down Europe's sidewalks belong to the upper-middle class, just as many statistics, and medals, make it clear that the runners with the most grit and tenacity are born on the Equator. Kenya, specifically, is now considered the Ithaca of running, the mecca of runners from all over the world, who go there in the hopes that, during a ten-day training course, the sun and heat of central Africa will transform them overnight into pale versions of Eliud Kipchoge, the long-distance marathon world-record holder.

The performances of African long-distance runners are so astonishing that they have led the sports community to speculate about their "racial advantage," even throwing into doubt the chances of someone without the same genetics achieving the same running times. There are many scientific studies about the phenomenon, and all of them focus on the incredible lung capacity and cardiovascular systems of runners who train in the shadow of Mount Kilimanjaro.

But as *Guardian* editorial columnist Adharanand Finn writes in his 2012 book *Running with the Kenyans*, these exceptional performances can't be attributed to DNA alone. To suss out the secret of Kenyan runners, the journalist spent over six months in Iten, a small town in Kenya rechristened the "running factory" for its concentration of medal winners and world-record holders. For weeks Finn ate only local food, ran barefoot, and did everything one would do when one is born in Africa and training for a marathon. But even after his African apprenticeship, his running time was still mediocre. Over the course of his experiment, Finn discovered that what fuels Kenyans' inexplicable talent isn't their muscles or lungs or hearts, but what, in its totality, running represents for them. In Kenya, running is a natural part of life, not a break from work and family. Indeed, for Kenyans, running is life itself, the one way to procure water, attend school, and occasionally improve their future.

Sadly, the rift between those who are born to run and those who are born to walk cannot be bridged. Given or denied, talent accepts no substitutes.

Yet this injustice doesn't take away from the dignity of people courageous enough to want to improve upon what they've been conceded, be it a little or a lot. That's what's most democratic about running: no matter how physically gifted you are, you cannot get around having to train regularly—and keep the faith occasionally. On the other hand, talent can quickly lead to arrogance and become dead weight.

Not infrequently, sheer tenacity makes up for bad running genes. And there are days when the designs of nature are overtaken, which Philostratus describes as "something wonderful, not to be talked about as a natural but as a rare phenomenon. You are seeing the work of a god who wanted to demonstrate something great to mortals."

All these big plans for gold and glory and now it's mid-June and I'm in bed with Covid! Talk about luck. I'd already gotten my first dose of the vaccine, already left for vacation on the French Riviera, and I was poolside at a party at the Cannes Film Festival when I received the text with my test results. I should try to be "positive" like the test says, but sometimes I just can't. To be honest, I almost never can.

This bad news has made me deathly allergic to the mere mention of the virus which for the last week has pervaded my body and all my conversations. I'm restricting myself to taking it like a sport, since sports is what I'm writing about, and note with bitterness that I am the posterchild for those with almost no chance of getting sick, according to the lunatics who have insisted and keep insisting on denying the serious of this illness: I'm young, athletic, and perfectly healthy. Yet here I am, in in bed with a fever.

Seven days have gone by without a run. That hasn't happened for at least a couple of years! Because of my health, obviously, which is making me feel more like a mollusk than a leopard at the moment, I've been unable to respond to this latest turn of events with my go-to phrase—I'm going for a run—and have had to replace the statement with a question: Should I go for a run?

*Although for now—and for the next few days I fear—
the answer is no, I'm reassured and consoled to confirm that
running has become the one reliable way for me to gauge
how I'm feeling, the means of measuring my strength and
stamina, for which, at the end of the day, I alone have to
answer, and pay.*

*Running has awarded me an accelerated degree in bodily
intuition, thorough knowledge of all my vital functions—
physical and psychic—and how they vary from context to
context. I started out corporal-illiterate, accustomed to
talking about my body and perceptions with childlike inac-
curacy and approximation. Ever since I began to run, "I'm
tired" has gone from being a generic phrase with which to
label every bad mood or momentary feeling of weakness, to
a specific statement that must be proven or disproven with
a pair of running shoes. Am I so exhausted that, if I go out
for a run, I'll fall asleep on the curb? Or is this vague sense
of tiredness all in my head, a weariness brought on by too
much thinking and feeling, so I might as well take it out for
a couple laps? It functions the other way around, too: "I'm
feeling fit." All right, then, but fit enough to run twelve
miles? Or is this passing euphoria good for just a couple of
sprints?*

*More importantly, now that I'm sick, my ability to gauge
how weak I am on my own enables me to accept it, take
ownership of it, and treat my feverish body and low spirits
with care. Knowing how "to feel" myself allows me to experience illness not as something alien or foreign to my body, as
something that exists just because a doctor diagnosed it, but
as something intimately mine, something I know deep down
in my bones and—crazy as it sounds—in my cells. Confined
to bed, rather than take them for granted or ignore them*

completely, I can sometimes sense my poor white blood cells as they struggle to resist the intruder and diligently produce antibodies, and I almost feel tenderly toward my body as it engages in this unjust, yet natural, war.

The Greeks had a word for this animal attachment to life: philozotéon, an adjective that means something like being a friend and ally to existence. Though for years I was my body's own worst enemy, the person most responsible for its aches and pains, thanks to running I now find myself cheering my body on, no longer rowing against the current and putting it in harm's way.

Finally I realize that the human body is programmed to struggle to keep living for as long as it can, within the natural limits of birth and death, alpha and omega. Before I took up running, I wasn't cheering on this inborn will to live; I was throwing stones at it from the bleachers. Now here I am, waving my arms and urging it to keep going. Or maybe that's the fever talking.

After spending half the summer training for my first marathon, I never would have guessed that one day I'd be saying, "I miss running." But now, after a week of forced immobility, God do I miss it. I miss the acuity, the unexpected sixth sense that running uncovered and honed. Not running, I'm aware that I don't know how I'm really doing. I don't know what the air at this time of year smells like. I don't quite know when the moon is waxing or waning in the summer sky. I don't know by heart the posters of the new movies and shows coming out in Paris, what progress the construction sites near my house are making, the particular green of the foliage. When I walk or go about my usual business, I don't even notice these things. Whereas when I run I am forced to *take careful note of everything that is going on both within me and without.*

I'll get it all back soon, of that I'm sure. Meanwhile, during this compulsory time out, I can't help but be grateful that running has become so much a part of me that, even when I don't run, I'm still somehow running. Even on days like today with my legs stretched out on the couch, some part of me is jogging along the Seine with the sun and wind in her face.

VII

In Corpore Sano

> Health is better than strength and beauty because health
> lies in the moist and dry, the hot and cold, in all the
> essential parts of the body, whereas strength and beauty
> lie in the secondary elements, in the muscles and bones
> and in a certain symmetry of the limbs.
> —ARISTOTLE, *Topics*, Book 3, Part I

Running represents a glaring anomaly in the landscape, unless that landscape is the woods or a race-
track. For both runner and onlooker, running defies
every rule and code of the civilized, urban, elegant lifestyle
that currently reigns in the West.

Running is the only sport—the only one I know of, anyway—for which you need nothing but can, and must, practice in plain view.

It may be true that, in the most extreme of cases, you
don't even need a pair of running shoes to run. But you
can't do without a road. And unless you own a castle or
a country estate, that road is open to the public, not re-
stricted to hardworking runners.

Every other sport requires traveling first, an initial
change of scenery—"I'm *going* to the tennis courts," "I'm
going to the pool," "I'm *going* to the dance studio"—that
signals a clear break from one's normal routine to concentrate on something else, usually within the walls of a
gym or a room or behind a fence, shielded from the pry-
ing eyes of those going about their daily routines, which
don't involve sports at all. Sure, you might happen upon

a soccer field, but you're probably not going to cross paths with someone practicing archery or working their abdominals at the office or supermarket. It's unlikely, that is, that sports will invade our space, unless we go looking for them.

Running works the other way around. To go out for a run you don't travel from one enclosed space to another but *step outside* the bounds of civilization. "I'm going out for a run," a phrase every runner uses, means crossing the threshold of polite society, which as a matter of decorum bars us from attending to our bodily needs in public, and visibly invading spaces where physical exercise is, as a rule, alien.

Though running has never put me personally in (really) embarrassing situations, we've all experienced that mix of surprise and shock upon bumping into a runner in places where, according to non-runners' rules of society, runners shouldn't be: on the beltway at the crack of dawn, out in the sun when it's 90 degrees in the shade, in the snow on Christmas Eve, in the parking lot of a shopping center on Saturday afternoon, on a path that leads to church. I've often seen runners bounding through the monumental cemeteries of Paris.

Runners know that, when they run, they break away from the indistinct mass of people who walk to life's little appointments and when they pick up their pace they become visible to the world. They not only know that; they want that.

It's undeniable. If we follow this line of thinking, running entails a healthy dose of exhibitionism. Which is why some people, even people in excellent physical shape, detest running and would willingly be crucified before running a yard in plain sight. They just can't do it.

*

No one can accuse runners of hiding—and why should they be confined to their own special park? And yet, with their tech accessories and neon attire, they make no effort to avoid drawing attention to themselves or blend in with the urban fabric. No, they want to be seen, they want to be recognized immediately as outliers proudly violating the routine feet dragging most people practice.

Here is where things break down: the runner wants to be seen by the sitter and the sitter has no wish to see him. I don't think I'm being perverse, at least no more than the average runner (I've asked around), when I confess that sometimes I take a subtle yet palpable pleasure in passing people seated at a bistro who have opted for French fries or a glass of wine instead of a pair of running shoes. To say nothing of the supreme affront of those who pair cognac with a smoke.

I know it's not big of me to derive strength from other people's weaknesses, weaknesses which were long my own and will go back to being so soon after I've finished the Athens Marathon, yet I can't help but want—need, rather—the stranger at the café enjoying his life to see me busy enjoying, or suffering through, my run. Not only do I want him to watch me sweating, gasping for breath, putting on my slightly ridiculous Olympic airs, as if running were a matter of life and death. I also want him to see the dignity in my effort and say, "Good for you."

I don't mean to punish people for indulging in a glass of wine at the end of the workday or a cream-filled croissant in the morning, but I do mean to show them there are alternatives. And I know they know it. I know by the way they watch me, by how they admire me—the kindest ones openly cheer and encourage me to keep at it. Not because of anything I'm doing—my times are laughable—but because of the almost religious respect that the spectacle of the human body in motion always earns from those who aren't moving. Or maybe underneath they resent me, maybe the fate of all runners is to wind up detested, even, in the end, taken for crazy, by people who don't run and are bothered by the exertion of runners.

Indeed, in that urban savanna where I run every morning, amid cars, scooters, buses, bicycles—even horses aren't a rare sight—what motivates me most aren't my supportive fellow runners but all those who have chosen not to run. Because they remind me so much of what I was like before I chose to run, and I don't like that image of myself. The prospect of going back to being the lazy—morally lazy, especially—person I used to be and abandoning the good habits that the more honest part of me recognizes are still tenuous and new so disturbs me that I'm driven to run even farther, even faster.

In the public sport that is running, in the precarious balance between seeing and being seen, lies my unhealthy past, which I'm afraid any false step could make visible to the outside world. Another reason I run is to get as far away as possible from it, to escape it.

* * *

"Health [hygiene in ancient Greek], they say, exists when the functions are in harmony with nature; wellbeing [*eutaxia*, literally good constitution] exists when all these functions enjoy a certain robustness. The common condition is that both are not ruled by illnesses; this state is also characterized by a body that functions perfectly well and resists dissolution." So writes Galen of Pergamum, one of the most noted physicians of antiquity—from whom we get the term galenic formulation, a practice of preparing drugs with several components—and author of a work called *Good Habits of the Body.*

I'm not a doctor, but ever since running has become one of my "good habits"—a surprising routine around which I schedule my day, on par with brushing my teeth, drinking coffee as soon as I'm up, or reading a few pages before bed—it's been unequivocal: a relentless tsunami of health has come crashing down on my life.

I'm still not clear as to which came first, whether starting to run steered me toward eating and sleeping better and taking scrupulous care of my health, or whether I suddenly became a glutton for turmeric and quinoa (one of my specialties) so that I could run a little longer the next day. However it happened, the result is the same. Until a few years ago I almost never ate breakfast, was the queen of cocktails on an empty stomach, and only regarded cooking as a good excuse to uncork a bottle of white wine, and today I lead a life according to a regimen so healthy and fastidious it makes an ashram look like a rave.

I'm not exaggerating. Not much anyway. Since I started to run my perception of my body's basic needs—what my body tells me to do so that I can go running again the next day—is so refined that I often wonder how I ever survived.

In my view, it's almost a miracle that I made it to thirty in a passable state of health after paying no real heed to what, on any given day, wound up on my plate, in my glass, or between my sheets. To be clear, I didn't live like a rockstar, and being born and raised in a part of the world blessed by the sea and a Mediterranean diet certainly helped give me strength and prolong my life even as I abandoned myself to the most recklessly sedentary behavior. Still, though I was never a fan of junk food, before running I never questioned whether my meals had a good balance of proteins and carbs. Sleeping was a chore to get over with as quickly as possible so that I could get back to the business of living and feeling things. To say nothing of cigarettes. Like Murakami, I quit cold turkey, not because I wanted to—I'd have continued smoking with impunity—but because tobacco prevented me from running to the best of my modest abilities.

Especially early on, when I would struggle to run a mile without stopping, my subconscious must have been compiling a list of activities that were counterproductive to running and, as a strategy to survive this (for me inane) effort, I stopped craving them. Tobacco was one of many things on that list. *On Gymnastics* is clear on this point: "Drinking wine, overeating, agitations of the soul and many other voluntary and involuntary things are harmful to sports." Like many coaches today, Philostratus advises against sex and sometimes even love—the greatest contributor to "agitations of the soul."

It may seem incredible—to me most of all—but my initial will to run was so keen that I was prepared to overcome any obstacle between me and running. I have no doubt that I would have killed the first person who dreamed of getting in the way of my completely trivial march toward becoming an athlete. When my old bad habits went up in smoke, new and much-needed ones emerged: from massaging my muscles with arnica to drinking ginger tea, from wearing running apparel—technical, yes, but sustainable—to eating granola and peanut butter bars.

All of a sudden my old pantry—that of a young single woman who turned her nose up at life and her own body—disappeared, replaced by a shelf of new provisions and a closet full of sportswear.

* * *

Reading Philostratus, I've come to see that I'm neither the first nor the only newcomer to sports to find herself perplexed by her increasingly healthy, balanced, organic, farm-to-table shopping list.

In *On Gymnastics* we find the following:

> Medicine was the first to tempt athletes with advice that, though useful, is often too squishy for sports, and teaches people to be lazy . . . Increasingly fatuous cooks have turned athletes into gluttons with bottomless appetites, proffering them indigestible poppyseed bread or food that runs contrary to the principles of gymnastics. They attribute to this or that fish natural properties based on information from far-flung seaside tribes, thus mud fish are heavy, shellfish tender, fish from the open sea meaty, fish from shallow waters lean, and fish that inhabit marshes delicate. They serve pork with a marvelous side of speeches, and their theories make people believe that groups of pigs that live by the sea are bad because of the sea garlic, of which the shoreline and the beach are full, and pigs that live near rivers are to be avoided because they consume crab. They say you should only eat pigs that subsist on acorns and berries. A life of such refined tastes may spell an exciting diet but leads one straight to the pleasures of Venus.

Clearly this epiphany that inspires people to make drastic changes to their routines and diets in the hopes of improving their health and performance must be common to any sport if for two thousand years every athlete has forgotten what up until the day before he had been used to eating as soon as he discovers sports.

If Philostratus is right and practicing sports inevitably leads people to pay more attention to the quality of what they consume so that they can transform it into energy, my own experience and the experience of the runners I know make me suspect that we may have taken things a bit too far; that this health kick has marked a seismic shift whereby every human being who dons a pair of running shoes is transformed into not only an athlete but a nutritionist, dietician, ecologist, and, sometimes, given the wide array of supplements and protein shakes out there, some sort of alchemist.

I'm not being the least bit ironic when I say that I am appreciative, proud even, of the way running has revolutionized my lifestyle, of which those fifty minutes a day that I tear down the pavement are but a small part. It is horrifying to think about letting junk disguised as nutrition freely course through my blood and making my poor cells work overtime to keep me standing and do what I want. Yet I can't hide the fact that I am often perplexed—shocked, really—when I see what ends up on my plate for the sake of this noble goal to "eat healthy." And it's not just on my plate. Frequently—I'd say almost every day in Paris (a city known for gourmet cooking)—I come across foods and drinks on menus or supermarket shelves that I'd honestly never heard of before.

Health foods, superfoods, exotic seaweeds, foreign spices, plant-based milk (soy or oat?), prepared goods from different continents, wholewheat bread with various amounts of yeast, fermented drinks, orange wines—the list of things that stun me has grown very, very long. No, I wasn't raised in the woods, and I love food from different cultures. What troubles me isn't the integration of all these foods into our diets but the principle embodied by this avalanche of foods old and new, local and exotic, that until recently were barely known and have now invaded our pantries. If they've made their way to us, it's because they're good for us, or better than all that stuff we were eating up until yesterday.

It's enough to scroll through our feeds or read one of the many magazines in circulation—even traditional newspapers now devote several pages to healthy living—to realize how many real and self-styled personal trainers have been elevated to the status of gurus advising us to eat the most peculiar foods, foraged or raised in the most unusual manners, and prepared in the weirdest ways possible, just like the fish Philostratus mentioned two thousand years ago. From ever-present proteins to the ubiquitous avocado, the health revolution is boldly underway in every corner of the world, especially on the plates and in the pantries of those who exercise every day. Clinging to my Italian passport, I thought I came from the country with the greatest culinary tradition in the world. I'd never have guessed that, in certain circles, sports circles and not, we're supposed to be embarrassed about ordering a pizza.

This hurricane of health enthusiasts has so changed the diets of athletes in the West and elsewhere that I wonder what our parents and grandparents' generation would think if they could see us now, thinking we're chic and willing to pay dearly for foods and drinks that twenty years ago were synonymous with poverty, or at least far from luxurious. Bread so whole it barely resembles a ciabatta or baguette, meat so lean you fear for the chicken's health, milk so artificial it's called "flavored," sweets made without sugar or yeast, unrefined grains, seeds and berries and nuts galore. In the blink of an eye those simple homemade meals our mothers lovingly raised us on seem obscenely low in nutrition and unbalanced. So much so that we suspect that they were trying to poison us by offering up butter and jam for breakfast, pasta with tomato sauce for lunch, breaded cutlets for dinner.

One aspect of this shift to organic food has given me particular pause: the triumph of eating "healthy" over craving what's "good." For centuries, millennia, rather, ever since the discovery of fire and the first cooked meals, when we stopped eating food ripped from the still-warm body of our prey, the development of human diets has been guided by the sense of taste alone. Anything not toxic or noxious was put to the age-old test of recipes and experiments, combined with thousands of different ingredients, which generated a vast wealth of gastronomical and anthropological culture, so that the best, richest, and tastiest variety of foods could be handed down to the next generation. The first indication that you had moved up the social ladder was that you ate better than the permanently under or malnourished lower classes and consumed larger portions of increasingly refined food—i.e., fatter and more succulent. Today this evolutionary trend seems to have been brusquely interrupted. No one, or at least no one who takes their health to heart, is interested in eating better tasting food. We all want to eat healthier food, and when it comes to our wellbeing we're willing to sacrifice taste.

By now the label "organic" (*biologico* or *bio* in Italian; literally: "biological") has replaced "high quality" in our stores, even for products that have nothing to do with food: from cotton shirts to hand soap, from the stuff we buy for our pets to toilet paper. Perhaps this means that, before earning their organic labels, those quality products weren't so quality. On the contrary.

In Greek "bio" meant neither good nor valuable. It wasn't even an adjective. *Bíos* meant life itself. In fact Greek possessed at least three words to express the miracle of being alive: *zoé* referred to an essence of life pertaining to all living beings, indiscriminately; to the miracle that separates what is living from stones and plastic. *Psyché* stood for vital spirit or lifeblood, the sense that one was fully alive, exactly the way I feel when, running, my breath quickens and my heart catches fire. And lastly there was *bíos*, which meant the conditions or ways in which life unfolds *nel mezzo del cammin*, to borrow Dante's phrase: what we choose to do with it, or how we waste it. If biology is the study of life, how have we come to consider, in the span of a few years, what is simply "naturally alive" to be commercially "good"? The rupture—the break—seems to be with the idea of introducing harmful, unhealthy and therefore lethal substances into our bodies—organic as opposed to artificial, then, vitality over death.

I have no doubt that Plato would be, at the very least, at a loss for words at this logical rift with which we seek to put *organic* foods on our plates and in our bodies, products without chemicals like pesticides and other poisons. Because the point is not our more than legitimate—a Greek would take it as a given—demand for naturally grown foods. The crazy thing is that for a long time we believed that the way the fields, seas, mountains, and rivers naturally yielded us their bounty could be circumvented, modified, perfected (as if it weren't already perfect) with technology and a great deal of arrogance. More specifically, for decades the natural world was asked to produce artificial foods, foods that, in normal conditions, it would never have produced. The recent wave of consumer wellness is really just an attempt to repair this deviation. But the generations making the attempt can't possibly remember what nature is, since they've never experienced it. We want an organic apple to be like an apple that a tree would naturally have produced rather than a ball of pesticides, yet none of us can recall what it was like before, when nothing was artificial and naturalness was a fact of life, not a supermarket sticker.

The same principle—the same lapse of memory—must lie at the root of the wellness obsession afflicting every runner I know. The point is not just to eat healthy but to relearn how to nourish the body and produce energy naturally, after decades of chemical supplements, miracle powders, creatine-injected muscles, and widespread levels of doping even among the most amateur of runners. Given that running is the one physical activity in our increasingly lazy and sedentary day, at least for me and everyone I know, this confusion about food is heightened; we belong to a generation of athletes for whom, to our shame, physical labor is neither a personal nor professional option. Indeed, for many people running is perhaps the activity on the calendar that burns the most calories. Except we no longer know where to go for the natural calories needed to run, hence the exotic foods, the fashions, the quirky tastes that Philostratus describes.

In ancient Greek the word "diet" doesn't mean watching what you eat or making sacrifices to lose weight. *Díaita* refers to a holistic approach to every aspect of your health, from food to sleep, from physical exercise to mental well-being. In this sense, running has rewarded me with the best possible diet and hygiene, in true Greek fashion. If I live longer or get sick less, it'll be thanks to sports alone.

And yet, though I feel a whole lot better, there remains a fundamental wrinkle, something closer to nostalgia than melancholy. Like a stain. I don't miss anything about those times when I ate and slept poorly, except for my carefree—mindless—attitude toward what was on my plate and, in general, toward taking a bite out of life.

Sometimes when I struggle to grasp what's going on around me, I get the nagging feeling that what we have gained from this health craze in wellbeing we have lost in joie de vivre and spontaneity. I doubt our attention to health, often transformed into obsession, will turn us into pleasure seekers. Or hedonists for that matter. Let's just hope Philostratus was right when he predicted the risk of indulging too much in the "pleasures of Venus."

It seems that, at least when it comes food, health takes precedence over pleasure because we no longer accept death. We want to feel well because we want to put off dying as long as possible, which is why we do everything we can to prevent any harm to our bodies.

That is perfectly dignified and legitimate. Any Greek athlete would be proud of us. But when we get so worked up about not getting sick, that voice murmuring in our ear that death is inevitable starts to get louder. It must be that deafening buzz that we all hear somewhere inside us as we work hard to stay healthy. This is the result of a normal transformation. We've gone from ridding death of its tragic sense to being generally afraid of getting old.

Look at us: out on the street, content to run another day, to stay healthy and young, to never have to face death one day.

* * *

One of the most fascinating aspects of the sport that keeps me from giving up on running and writing is my confidence that, after studying ancient Greece for years, I have finally found something in common with the Greeks, something undeniable and concrete, something that hasn't been changed by the passing of time and enables me to feel today exactly what they felt two thousand years ago: the human body.

Maybe everything has changed since the days when Plato and his companions strolled the streets of Athens philosophizing: technology, science, literature, religion, political and economic ideologies, not to mention the language, which is called "dead" because no one speaks it. But not the human body. That hasn't changed one iota—or one cell. Because the nucleotides that make up the chains of our DNA have not undergone any alterations, my muscles, lungs, heart, etc. are identical to those of a fifth-century Greek (except mine aren't nearly as strong) and the fatigue, euphoria, determination, dejection, and hilarity that I feel every time I go out for a run on the streets of Paris are exactly the same that every human being in history has felt while running, wherever in the world they happen to have been.

This thought, which never ceases to pique my curiosity about the universal and continuous act of running, prompts another. The theater in which men and women ran in the past hasn't changed either. Nor will it in the future. Earth has remained the same; living on another planet seems unthinkable for now. Like two thousand years ago, we have yet to organize races in unknown galaxies. What has changed, and changed for the (much) worse, is the health of our planet, which has suffered at the hands of human neglect, arrogance, and greed, and been reviled by economic policies that worship at the altar of exploitation.

The environmental crisis represents a side of modern running that would have been completely foreign—inconceivable—at the time of the Greek Olympics, when life was designed *within* nature, not pitted against it. Clearly Philostratus didn't feel the need to mention the environment in which sports were played, because for him—and his fellow ancients—it was taken for granted, not worthy of mention, certainly not a phenomenon to analyze and preserve. Besides, the word ecology is, like nostalgia, a modern borrowing from ancient Greek, a word that sounds Greek but isn't. A word for the scientific study of the relationships between living organisms and their environment wasn't coined until 1866, by the German biologist Ernst Haeckel, and combines two ancient Greek words: *ōikos* ("home" or "surroundings") and *logos* ("speech").

The health craze that has revolutionized how we eat is in large part motivated by the environmental crisis. There's no sense in pretending to lead a healthy lifestyle on a sick planet. Likewise, it's impossible for a sick planet to produce healthy food. The need to reduce our so-called ecological footprint, the exact toll our consumption takes on the planet, has driven numerous citizens and companies to take better care of the environment, starting with what winds up on our dinner tables, promoting vegetables or thinking up new alternatives to steak and potatoes. But until recently I wasn't aware of the anxiety about the environment presently gripping the running world. Stupidly, I thought that running was among the most sustainable sports in the world and that it had nearly no impact on the environment, because in my mind runners consume only energies that they produce, asking nothing of their environment except for an honest exchange of oxygen for carbon dioxide—not the fairest bargain, given the shameful levels of urban pollution that we breathe in in lungfuls as we run behind cars and mopeds.

More and more runners are calling for frank conversations concerning the environment, foremost among them the organizers of major marathons, which can hardly be called eco-friendly. True, those twenty-six miles of road are public and don't require significant construction work. Yet getting thousands of athletes from one part of the globe to another just to have them run isn't great for the environment. According to data from a 2016 racing forum in France, at least one quarter of nearly 17 million French runners participated the year before in an organized competition —and not always in their own backyards.

This new environmental awareness has also driven sporting goods companies to rethink the materials they use for producing shoes and garments, which can't be made with non-recyclable plastic much longer, and the makers of dietary foods and supplements to put something better than low-quality synthetic proteins and amino acids in their bars and drinks.

Surely it's just me, as it was when I spoke of the recent health craze, but every once and a while—most of all when

I'm in a shopping center—I suspect this trend is yet another marketing campaign to sell more rather than consume less. Still, I'll happily welcome any change that can shift contemporary society away from its extraction or "taker's" mentality and toward human beings and the environment that until recently we took for granted.

More than anything running has taught me that *nature* exists—I mean concretely, not as some abstract idea divided into even more abstract seasons.

Running is the most contemplative activity there is. Once upon a time people considered it a mystical form of pilgrimage. Finally at a remove—freed—from the thousands of daily distractions, we're left to contemplate only two landscapes when we run: the interior landscape of emotions and physical sensations, and the exterior landscape of streets, trees, rivers, and, for those lucky enough, mountains and seas.

Apart from the (in my opinion) unnatural practice of running indoors on a mechanical treadmill, the sport finds its raison d'être in the environment where it gets done. Even if we no longer run for rational reasons—to get from one place to another—runners always pass through nature.

And because I for one find it very hard to spend an hour concentrating on my inner world, probing deeper and deeper, like a speleologist, to unearth something of interest, why not have a look around? Whether gazing at pristine parks—the most worthwhile running experience—or concrete slabs—the most frustrating—the runner's eye learns to observe and love its surroundings, which is the one way to respect them.

Indeed running is one of the few activities that restores

human beings to their rightful place, getting them off the couch or out from behind a desk and placing them back in the environment where they came into this world many millennia ago: nature.

It isn't just about admiring trees and the countryside but reawakening and retraining the senses. Increasingly shackled to the comforts of our domestic walls and phone screens, we drown out our sense of hearing with noise-cancelling earplugs, clog our sense of smell with artificial deodorants, anesthetize our sense of touch with lotions and sunscreens. When you run, the wind strikes your face and finally you feel it! You breathe in its scent, you feel the cold slipping under your shirt or the warmth caressing your bare arms at the start of summer. Your sense of hearing doesn't just function to absorb the beats of a playlist, but to listen out for the danger of traffic and pedestrians, ever slower and more distracted. Your sense of sight functions to keep an eye out for the finish line.

Forcing me to concentrate on what's going on around me, not just inside me, running has given me the rare gift of feeling like a part of nature rather than someone admiring the view high up on a balcony. And maybe for the first time my brain has gone back to doing what it was programmed to do from the age of the first homo sapiens: cataloging the outside world—nature—and keeping an eye out for threats and prey instead of wearily scanning the endless fields of its own thoughts, where the only thing that's real and palpable is our own stress.

Up until the 1960s, the very few joggers who trotted across the parks of their cities were considered crazy. When not practiced strictly as a sport, running was seen as a bizarre, totally unusual hobby and often regarded with

suspicion. Athletics, physical exercise generally, were reserved for clubs and federations, cut off from the world,
practiced inside stadiums and fields. Sports were the narrow domain of elites and not done on your own, improvis-
ing outside your front door.

It's weird to think the running boom that began in the
1960s was originally championed by hippies. We tend to
picture flower children as smoking weed at reggae concerts
rather than sweating on the street in a pair of sneakers. But
the ones who initially reclaimed an individual's right to
stretch her legs where and when she pleased belonged to the
counterculture movements that grew out of 1968. Indeed,
running became a clarion call for freedom that combined
environmentalism and feminism. Finally, besides being lib-
erating, running also had a mystical side that wasn't lost on
hippies, either, who saw how running regularly could be a
gateway to other dimensions, just as psychedelic as drugs
but less damaging—beneficial, actually—to one's health.

Because I almost always run the same route, I know almost every tree in Montmartre. Because I observe them
almost every day, I assess their transformation over the seasons, which have become a concrete experience for me as
the leaves and flowers change, and not just an abstract idea
organized by holidays: Christmas, summer vacation, etc. If
I have to go out after a run, I know exactly whether it's hot
or cold, whether I have to bring a sweater or an umbrella,
without having to check the weather app on my phone.

Spending so much time out of doors has made the
changes in temperature and atmospheric pressure seem
friendly, their cycle natural, no longer irrelevant nuisances
to suppress by blasting the heater or air conditioner.

"There's no such thing as bad weather, just soft people,"

said co-founder of Nike and track and field coach Bill Bowerman. Like it or not, I have to agree. Running has shown me that there is rarely a rain so hard that I can't find time for a run. When I began running, I was soft and sensitive to the cold, and being caught off guard by a cold snap was my greatest fear. Every gray sky on the horizon was a good excuse to skip a workout. But as I continued to run I came to realize that steady rains that last twenty-four hours only exist in the dark and stormy cloud of weather icons. Not even on gloomy November days have I had to miss a run because of a prolonged rain; putting it off a few hours has always been enough to find at least a twenty-minute window of dry weather, even on the gloomiest of days. I could say the same of the heat, wind, or shortest days of the year, when it's already dark out by the early afternoon. Running has taught me to be more patient, more flexible, and occasionally more imaginative.

Running has even changed my view of the city. I know my neighborhood better than Google does, my photographic memory of stores and restaurants has become as unwavering as the confidence with which I change up my route or explore a street I've never been down before. Turning every stimulus into a mental pastime, I know exactly what's opening at the movie theater and the theater, I see what's on display in the stores or on sale at the supermarket, and sometimes I make a mental note of bistros I want to check out.

I have also had the pleasure of running in cities that I happened to be passing through for the first time, for work or on vacation. Discovering them that way was priceless, freeing me from the tyranny of top-ten-must-see lists, and the feeling, after just a few miles, that these cities were in a sense my own came as a huge surprise. No wonder you can now find blogs specializing in slow tourism for curious runners on the move.

It's not all that bucolic—of that I'm perfectly aware. Just as I'm aware that being a fan of running won't change the world. But it will make you a little more courteous and respectful. Feeling part of your environment gives you the best chance of going from clients to inhabitants, and therefore of looking after the home inscribed in the word "ecology."

Running inevitably makes people more demanding: runners not only want to stay healthy but expect a healthy environment in which to workout. No runner is going to roll over when her neighborhood park or river trail is converted into parking lots or infested with trash. Athletes are prepared to put up a fight so that the air that they breathe is just that—breathable—and their surroundings don't look like a heavily-trafficked highway.

This doesn't mean taking the kind of radical stances championed by activist runners who believe the one way to respect nature is to run in your neighborhood and avoid making superfluous, environmentally unfriendly trips. For many people, myself included, running represents a first, much-needed step toward adopting a sustainable lifestyle, which doesn't translate to a revolution so much as to a considerateness toward the world we run in—a form of radical respect for ourselves, others, and the environment. We make an eco-friendly choice every time we put on our sneakers.

* * *

In addition to the health and sustainable living revolutions, a wave of new technology has rocked the world of running, and sports in general. According to data collected by the 2016 forum, seventy-two percent of runners may run alone, yes, but they always have a device on them.

Gone are the days of digital watches and devices for listening to music or podcasts. For the past few years we have started taking the measure of everything in every way possible. Armed with innumerable gadgets, present-day runners look more like stars in a dystopian movie than athletes from ancient Greece who trained in the buff, equipped with nothing but their muscles.

On my first runs, all I took with me was my smartphone with one of the many free apps that only measure distance, speed, and incline. Six months later, no longer a weekend runner, I had become a slave to my brand new smartwatch, which recorded everything about my miserable, exhausted body: not just external data, like how many miles I'd run or the pace I'd kept, but the effect of the run on my organs, from my heartbeat to the maximum amount of oxygen I use per minute, the so-called VO2max, a metric of your cardiorespiratory fitness and aerobic capacity (it measures your ability to deliver oxygen from the lungs to other parts of your body and turn it into energy) which has become a kind of oracle of every athlete's performance—something I had no idea existed the day before. Combining these and a thousand other bits of data, the algorithm for modern watches can establish your biological age (as opposed to your chronological age), your margin of improvement, how much you need to train to achieve peak performance, your fitness level, and the right speed for a recovery run.

And to think that in ancient Greece the one thing that could be measured and monitored was your breath (data that was easily demonstrable). "The limit of exercise is labored breathing," writes Galen, ignoring the difference between aerobic and anaerobic exercise. "Hence movements that do not cause your breathing to change do not deserve to be called exercise." Thanks to technology, our current practice of measuring everything in sports has turned into an obsession with manipulating players' performances, inspiring coaches to recreate every weather condition and variable in their gyms so that they can see how athletes react to them using algorithms so sophisticated that you start to wonder whether they're testing athletes or machines. One of the latest examples of technology's supremacy was the recent 2020 Games in Tokyo. 2,797 years after the first Olympics, athletes were ready to take on the hot and humid climate of Japan after months of training in facilities where they could reproduce the altitude, humidity, and oxygen levels of the place where they would ultimately compete.

While technology can monitor an athlete's every movement, engineers, for their part, have turned their attention to sports equipment. Look no further than running; the old flat-soled running shoes with which Emil Zatopek set the world record in the 1950s are laughable by today's standards. Beginning in the 1970s, major sportswear companies had a literal field day coming up with high-tech solutions to meet the needs of athletes, first with their form-fitting outfits and then with shoes, cranking out increasingly sophisticated models made with cushioning materials, the fruit of meticulous research done by physicists and chemists.

Exciting as some of the stories surrounding the making

of these sneakers may be, I'm a bit bothered by the consequences of the latest footwear thought up by Nike and copied by other brands. This footwear "with a platform," so-called for its inner foam that sits on a carbon fiber plate, guarantees runners at least a 1.5% advantage and is responsible for a flurry of new records. In March 2021, forty-two runners at the Tokyo marathon wore these expensive sneakers and crossed the finish line in under two hours and ten minutes, an astonishing feat. The Japanese runner Kengo Suzuki became the first man not born in Africa to shatter the two-hour and five-minute barrier.

Of course I launched headfirst into this frenzy of hi-tech sportswear, just as I had with healthy-living and diet fads. For months I scoured magazines, advertisements, and newsletters to keep up with the latest big brand news and purchase the most futuristic shoes, and each time I did I'd be surprised to discover that I needed something else, something that in my ignorance I had been doing without (though I had survived).

To be clear, I wasn't under the illusion that I was going to shatter any glass ceilings thanks to a pair of hi-tech running shoes. That would have taken a miracle. But I felt proud to be a part of a marketing niche, a small and exclusive world that I'd joined by running and that did nothing but study physics, chemistry, and biology so that I could run better and longer. I'd been hypnotized by advertising, which made me think a new pair of shoes could bring me closer to transitioning from an amateur who runs in whatever's lying around the house into a pro, a champion with a whole line of innovative and high-performing bespoke outfits.

Far less exciting were the gadgets that I strapped to my wrist. They felt more like psychological shackles than something that would unlock my athletic potential. Clearly the problem stemmed from my inflexible character and natural inclination to play by the rules. There were times when I would go out for a run just to keep my smartwatch from yelling about how it couldn't believe I hadn't met the workout goals it had set for me. I was cowed by its annoying notifications urging me to take more steps than I had the previous day; by its monthly and annual reports on my training progress, which trended downward and made me feel like a failure; by its absence of limits, so that, even if I ran twelve miles one day, I was ready and willing to push myself to run even farther the next.

I'm sure these notifications, individual and group challenges, reminders, and graphics are excellent motivation for the wishy-washy. But not for me. They stress me out. They make me feel inadequate and guilty whenever I glance at my smartphone—which, in the end, I happily started to ignore, newly liberated and master of my own runs.

Now I run in whatever clothes I feel like—some mornings I even run in the shirt I slept in—armed only with my smartphone, which I use discreetly to measure my speed and distance, nothing else (and sometimes, if the battery's dead, not even that). It may not be the perfect or most orthodox training method, but it works for me. Rather than the threats of a watch, I prefer to trust more homespun and less universal parameters to evaluate a workout, like how I feel before, after, and during a run, and then adjust the pace to what physical shape I'm in or the mood of the day.

Besides, technology or not, one of the great lessons that

running has taught me is to stop laboring under the illusion that I ought to correct myself or others as if personal progress were constant. Running has shown me that there are limits and it is within those limits that one has a physical and moral obligation to try to improve oneself.

I f I had to say how many times I've gone out for a run when I didn't want to, I'd have to conclude approximately every time.

Even this morning I didn't want to put on my running shoes and hit the streets. It's been three years since I caught the running bug, yet I still feel a lingering discomfort. I have the impression—certainty—that I am a person of privilege, that I'm all worked up about something superfluous, unnecessary, and, at the end of the day, completely pointless. But I still went out today. I didn't want to. I needed to.

Because I have little—i.e., no—interest in strengthening my calves, they don't look much different from when they were squeezed between the legs of a desk. A little shapelier, maybe, but not prizewinners. I think I'd have given running up after my first failed outing were it not for the mental wellbeing it provides. Ever since my first sallies down the street, I was shocked by this intense, consistent relief from the pressures and anxieties of daily living. I had never felt anything like it before. Even the effects of benzodiazepine pale in comparison to a half-hour run. I imagine that athletes will find all this as ordinary as discovering hot water, but for me running was a total revelation, and it has turned out to be necessary for a whole host of reasons, among which my physical shape is the least important.

I was thinking about it again this morning when, at mile three, I turned down the canal near the Place de la Bastille and suddenly felt more alive and determined than a revolutionary about to decapitate a king. My muscles may say no every day, but my imploring, grateful head pleads with me to answer yes.

For me there's no greater joy, at least as concerns running, than doing what I did today: darting down the streets of Paris with a "mindful-running" podcast in my ears, braving the cold winds and soupy weather of a late summer day in France. Almost all the major sportswear running apps now offer guided runs with a mindfulness coach. The one I used today paired the voice of a coach with the teachings of a mindfulness expert (i.e., not too transcendental, not too pedantic).

I'm so fascinated by these training programs that I sometimes I wonder whether they're the real reason I run: to meditate while in motion. Besides the principles they've taught me, which can be quickly gleaned from any mental health advice column—the importance of living in the moment, of relinquishing control, of treating myself and others with care and patience—the pure pleasure that mindfulness training gives me has had an excellent and tangible effect on parts of my life that take place after I've removed my sneakers. Maybe my muscles haven't changed much since my lounging around days. But my neurons have. A lot. My mind is the part of my body that running has most honed, not my legs, so much so that I wonder why on earth I never ran before and, more importantly, why doesn't everyone run.

Though you can't tell it by looking at me, this mental preparation is what I'm most proud of about my new life as a runner, and it may be why I keep running. It's not just a question of feeling well or at peace; running improves my focus and working memory whatever I happen to be doing. Including when I'm at rest. As for my muscles, like I said: they're not my real concern. If I run, it's also to discover how far I can push myself to give my brain a workout, how agile and quick it can become if I leave it free to wander, as I do when I run, and not yoke it to books and dictionaries.

Mental weightlifting aside, ever since I was taken with the idea to write about running, one thing has, unfortunately, proved undeniable: running has become more and more of a burden. I enjoy it a lot less, and I need it a lot more.

It's as though running has spilled over into every aspect of my life, and I can't stand it anymore. Not only has running hijacked all my conversations. Not only do my friends keep asking me when I'm going to run the marathon in Athens (the date is fast approaching). Not only do I do nothing but read books and articles about it. But, worst of all, running has gotten in the way of my writing, and vice versa, in a vicious and exhausting circle that I don't know how to break.

If I got out for a run, it's to think about running and then write about it. Once I've written, I have no energy left and need to go out for another run to find new inspiration. Running had once been my escape from obligations and overthinking, a freedom I never shared with anybody. Now the street has become my notebook where I jot down ideas to share with readers.

There are days, like this morning, when the American accent of my mindfulness coach blasting through my earbuds does the trick and I arrive home reinvigorated, buoyed, ready to sit down and write again. Then there are days when I feel like chucking the podcast and its Zen wisdom, along with whatever I'm writing, into the Seine.

My restlessness must be a product of inexperience. I've never been so free on the page, so open, at so far a remove from my previous work, and I've not even run a marathon yet. In my darker moments, I alternate between dreams of giving up writing for good once I'm done with this project and dreams of giving up running. Or of giving up both.

For now, I'm hanging in there, I think. I go out to run so that I can write, and I write so that I can run. It sounds funny, but that's my life at the moment, and, like everybody else, I'm doing my best to keep my balance.

VIII
KALOS KAGATHOS: AESTHETICS AND RUNNING

> A respectable man is characterized by health,
> beauty, and the ability to run.
> —PLATO, *The Republic*

Sometimes I wonder if running is just a desperate attempt to outstrip pain. Of one thing I'm certain: those of us who insist on lacing up our running shoes in the morning are serious masochists.

In canto 3 of the *Inferno*, Dante, horrified by the groans he hears in hell's anteroom, asks Virgil: "Master, what pain is it / that makes these souls cry out so loud?" People running, his guide replies. Virgil is referring to the pusillanimous souls, the uncommitted, those who failed to side with good or evil and are now condemned for eternity to chase after a white flag, a symbol of their cowardly indecision.

Running is the first punishment in hell that readers of the *Divine Comedy* encounter. The condemned look so desperate that Dante calls them *gent' è che par nel duol sì vinta* (people defeated by pain). Having lived with "neither disgrace nor honor," they now must run forever, naked and aimless, while bees and horseflies sting their flesh and disgusting worms swallow their blood and tears. Petulant, dithering, the pusillanimous souls are so intolerable not even Satan wants them in hell, and Virgil urges Dante "not to talk about them but look and pass on."

This scene in the *Commedia* isn't so different from the chilling spectacle of a modern-day marathon, minus the nasty horseflies and with an inch or two more of clothing.

For those who run regularly, watching a non-Olympic marathon is like watching collective suicide: a human apocalypse where the tired and dazed participants willingly punish themselves.

Anyone who happens to be out on the streets of New York or Rome or Paris during the annual Sunday marathon will witness several thousand individuals of all ages and provenances passing by, often in a hard rain or arctic cold, and aside from the handful of professional runners for whom 26.2 miles is a breeze, all of them look as if they are marching to their deaths and may very well die of exhaustion just like the first marathon runner in history. Some runners vomit, others double over. Some try to massage away the cramps in their calves, others the stabbing pains in their sides. Some cry, others pray. Almost no one looks happy to be running, reinforcing something Emil Zatopek, a runner famed for his grimace, once said: "I was not talented enough to run and smile at the same time."

Also in the annals of running is the tenacious, determined Gabriela Andersen-Schiess, whose pain tolerance was almost superhuman. At the 1984 Los Angeles Olympics the Swiss long-distance runner lurched across the finish line, staggering from dehydration, before collapsing unconscious into the arms of medics. The deeply affecting images of the incredible pains she took to finish circulated the globe, inciting a lot of debate over the cruel physical suffering on full display. (When I rewatched the scene online, I almost cried.)

Plato and the Greeks spilled a lot of ink about the inherent beauty of sports and the elegance of accepting pain and the aesthetic glory to be found in sweat and dust. Maybe what they had to say is true, though I myself have never felt uglier than when on a run: red-faced, wet-haired, with mud spattered across my calves when it's raining and sweat pouring down my back when it's sunny. Running is the opposite of ideal beauty. At the end of a workout, I'm dragging myself through the lobby of my building and ardently praying that no one sees me.

Running doesn't involve grace. Elegance maybe, for the few people fortunate to have a natural stride, but the act of pushing the human body to its physical limit strips away all traces of serene beauty. And it's on account of this pain, as intolerable as it is manageable, that we so love to run.

Asked about what makes running a marathon a mystical experience, nobody would start by listing the beauty of the city they ran in or the kindness of their fellow runners or the effectiveness or not of the race's design or the quality of the rest areas. Drily and succinctly, everyone describes how they suffered like dogs. It's the thing they like best, and the reason they keep at it. No one would run a marathon if it was easy, pleasant, and painless.

Especially now that we're a few weeks away from the Athens Marathon and in addition to coming up short of breath I feel like I'm spitting my lungs out, like every cell of my miserable body is thinking "I can't take it anymore!" what most comforts me and keeps me going is the knowledge that I chose this pain: I knew it, I wanted it, I asked for it. And I'm ready to swear on the old slogan "no pain, no gain."

So runners suffer, and a marathon is really hell's anteroom (Dante describes it so well one wonders if he himself weren't a runner). No one is hiding the fact that running is hard work. Not only is there no hiding the pain, but pain is the point, the flag that runners bear. If you don't feel pain, if you don't embrace it, then you're not really running.

Therefore, in running, pain is sought out, selected, put on display. Only after that does it turn to gold and glory.

The Greeks expressed their physical and moral ideal with just one word: *kalokagathia*, a combination of the adjectives *kalos* and *agathos* that, put very briefly, means "good and beautiful."

I remember translating dozens of texts in high school where this ancient blend of virtue and beauty appeared and never quite grasping its meaning. The rote translation sounded admissible to my ear yet far from the mark. I could apprehend the idea that morality was inherently connected to beauty, but that was about it, since I had yet to build my own aesthetic categories. And if the beholder finds unquestionably beautiful that which is good because virtuous, then all Greeks were beautiful to me. Homer may have been blind and Socrates far less beautiful on the outside than on the in, according to his description in the *Symposium,* but the sublime nature of their works made me picture them all as blonds, as attractive and muscular as the stars of American movies set in and around Troy.

I had long believed that to achieve the ideal encapsulated in *kalos kai agathos* you had to have written the *Iliad* or been the first to name the planets in our galaxy or sculpted the Parthenon or invented a philosophical system from scratch. Or at least have given your life at Thermopylae to win a war for your people. I thought that anyone who hadn't reached the heights of Homer, Plato, or Pythagoras should be relegated to the other side of the field, the side reserved for the *kakos kai aischros,* the ugly and bad, toward which I myself was quickly headed, as was anyone who hadn't had the luck to be born in Athens in the fifth century.

But then, while training for my first marathon and writhing like one of the damned, I realized that for twenty years I had been living inside the "heads" of the Greeks, grappling with their language, their poetry, their philosophy, and the long list of wonders produced by their extraordinary neurons. But I had forgotten that they also had bodies, that they were made of flesh and blood, that they had impulses and desires and bodily needs. In my desperate attempt to emulate Philippides, I came to see that putting myself in the shoes of the ancients was a worthy endeavor. Because if it's true you must exercise your brain to achieve *kalokagathia*, it is equally true that you must exercise your muscles. Maybe the muses alone won't inspire an epic poem. It also takes quick feet and strong calves.

In *Timaeus*, Plato writes, "People who devote themselves to scientific research or other intellectual pursuits must exercise and practice gymnastics, while people who focus on their physical fitness must also furnish their souls with the proper motions and study music and philosophy if they hope to be called truly beautiful and truly good." A little later he goes on to add that sports are the best "vehicle for the soul."

Evidently, and shockingly, this point had eluded me until I put on a pair of running shoes. For years I had allowed my soul to pursue its "proper motions," as Plato has it, a few recklessly so, but not my legs. Those I had kept comfortably tucked under my desk or stretched out on a sofa. I used to rack my brains staring up at the statues of Greek athletes and heroes, groping at ideas about harmony and symmetry, when I was the one off-balance, a slave to sitting still, which didn't sharpen my mind but made it limp. Now I know that as I looked up at the *Discobolus* I should have been concentrating on his abs of steel rather than on the golden ratio and his air of contrition.

As I've said time and again in this book, this failure must have been due to my never having been taken by the hand and guided down the path of sports. But it doesn't help that our education and labor systems expect us to sit for over a third, if not half, the day. With all the hours I sat studying at a desk, I'm afraid a hundred marathons wouldn't make up for the sad sedentary state in which I spent three decades of my life. The first lyceum in history, founded by Aristotle in the temple of Apollo Lyceus (whence the name), was called peripatetic after the long philosophical discussions held while in motion, with teachers and students intently walking. The word, which would later define Aristotelian thought, comes from *peripatoi*, meaning "the pillars of the porticoes" in the Athenian gymnasium, where young people exercised. To this day, in various languages, the word "gymnasium" can refer to a sports gym, as in Spanish, and a prep school—the so-called gym of letters—as in Italian or French.

Centuries later, Michel de Montaigne wrote in his *Essays*, "My thoughts sleep if I sit still; my mind doesn't budge unless my legs move it." As the upstanding, lazy offspring of Judeo-Christian culture, I'd always believed the body and spirit were discrete entities, and that of the two the latter was superior. My mind, as per Montaigne, must have been slumbering on all those chairs where I willingly deposited myself. For decades I thought a Greek dictionary (which I carried under my arm because it was too big to keep in my backpack) was more valuable than a gym bag, and I mistakenly thought that having read many books I possessed the most developed and chiseled mind in my neighborhood. Now I know it was just the most cluttered and neurotic.

Because of my unforgivable, childish ignorance, until a couple of years ago the mere idea of running a few yards—an action I regarded as equal parts absurd and pointless—would have made me laugh. Nowadays it seems so obvious and natural that, in some ways, training for a marathon appears to be the most Greek activity I've ever pursued, far more than the texts I've studied and translated.

It is only now that I realize that the languages we call dead, because they are only spoken in our heads, require a precision and rigor unheard of in our raucous, sloppy day and age. The same goes for sports, which depend solely on the biological functions of our muscles and require a care, devotion, and discipline that can't be circumvented. And just as learning ancient Greek or Latin takes time—*years*—and devotion and sacrifice, so, too, does playing soccer or swimming at a professional level.

No doubt the comparison will strike you as ridiculous and naïve, but in my experience, the workouts—which I carefully plan and never improvise—that led to my first half-mile run without a break, then my first three, six, ten, twenty, and so forth, and that in a few weeks will get me through my first marathon, aren't so different in terms of effort, devotion, and ambition, from the intellectual exercises that took me from copying out the Greek alphabet in a shaky hand to learning (a bit sadistically) grammatical paradigms by heart, from translating a single sentence to a short text, from Plato's prose to chapters of the *Iliad* and *Odyssey* (a personal highpoint).

By choosing to move "my spirit" and learn Greek and Latin first and my legs second, I may be doing things backwards. However, now that I'm unexpectedly hard at work training for a marathon, the discipline that I learned thanks to ancient letters—how to keep myself, my weaknesses, and my ambition in check—is what inspires and sustains me every morning I run along the Seine.

And even if my running time from Marathon to Athens will be risible, at least my body and spirit will finally exist, as Plato suggests, in harmony. I can't aspire to break an Olympic record, but I can achieve my share of *kalokagathia*.

At least I have found (another first) a practical answer to offer people who ask me what's the point of studying ancient literature. It may have been a long time coming, but plainly my studies have helped me train for a marathon.

* * *

Now I see clearly what this mysterious thing called mental health is made of, that which all runners, first to last, regard as the holy grail of footracing. It's relief from the mind's relentless, aggravating chatter.

From a biological point of view, running chiefly entails dominating your body so that it submits to your will, making it endure long distances and triumph over our natural state of rest. Whatever our underlying reasons for running—immortal glory for ancient champions, Olympic records for their modern counterparts, and for the rest of us losing weight or staying healthy—the practice is firstly about testing our bodies, forcing them to work harder than they would by simply walking. Walking won't do, because walking doesn't cause the kind of pain needed to transcend our state of rest.

You suffer when you run because your body would happily sit still. That's why, as a counter measure, your mind takes pleasure in it. Your legs move and your thoughts stop racing, as if under a spell. Finally, for once, your consciousness sits still! Not all runners are perverse masochists, as pedestrians might reasonably think when they see us galloping in the rain. There's pleasure in the act of running, but you won't find it in your legs. It's in your head. Running a marathon, your muscles move for 26.2 miles and your mind is still. Four-plus hours of ungodly exertion: numb calves, shortness of breath, a racing heart. But also four-plus hours of peace of mind, one's anxieties at last silent, the distinct sense of oneself and the concrete underfoot.

Running is hard, sometimes very hard, but the peace of mind it affords is unequalled. The price of that peace depends on how willing we are to stretch our bodies to obtain it.

Our bodies ache, our minds are at ease. It isn't so different from the opposite situation, when we're physically motionless at our desk, but our brain is fuming as it ferrets out an idea or chases after some project. The inverse is also true: when something doesn't make sense or we're troubled by an idea, we might as well take it outside for a walk and stretch our neurons in the hope that, by tiring ourselves out, our worries or uncertainty will abate. It's a bit like when, absorbed in complicated thoughts, we pace the hall or circle a table endlessly.

I believe that's what Plato meant. To think well, we ought

to run, to air our ideas, to keep from spinning our wheels. And to play sports, now and then we need to stretch out on the couch with a good book.

Compared to the many sports characterized by other attributes—team spirit, competitiveness, the thirst for victory, the relationship with nature—the pleasure of running is much less physical and far more psychological. No wonder only one-third of the 17 million French runners say they run for physical pleasure, according to data from the 2016 racing forum. I too can think of a thousand other more creative and congenial ways to make my legs happy without making them run for miles. Yet to attain the mind-body balance that running repays, runners the world over are willing to hit the streets, no matter how bad the weather or how busy their schedules, so that they can winkle out some peace from their ankles.

It only now occurs to me that our legs are just the instrument, the means with which we run, while our muscles aren't very involved in the enterprise. People don't run to work out their calves. They run to free their minds. From the time of Philippides's marathon to today, and every Olympics in between, runners have been searching for something far different from the road than happy feet. And in every movie from *Chariots of Fire* to *Forrest Gump* running is always a means of arriving somewhere else, a place where our ideas and values can at last breathe.

Controlling the body to free the spirit, making your legs ache so that your mind can smile, that's how you achieve running bliss. Perverse—and no doubt complicated—as it may sound, running is the best method for making peace with life that I've ever known. It can seem like a

Dantean-level form of corporal punishment, but the good it does our minds is close to heaven.

* * *

Now that we've located where this mental wellbeing that makes all runners a bit more *agathos* comes from, let's look at *kalos*, the other half of the equation, and shift our focus to the aesthetic side of running, to a phenomenon that would make Plato shudder: people who put themselves through the paces in order to feel "beautiful" and could care less about the intellectual side of the endeavor.

Are runners beautiful? Do they correspond to our modern ideal of physical beauty? I don't think so. And yet today there's almost no one more fashionable, no one cooler, than a runner. That she be the slowest lumberer on Earth to have pounded the pavement doesn't matter.

Long-distance runners don't have "beautiful" bodies. They have functional ones. Wiry, slim, they exercise to eliminate anything that won't help them run. And in running, every pound of excess fat is like humping a pound of rocks on your back. That said, thin though they may be, runners look nothing like the models that the media proposes. They have barely visible muscles, toothpicks for legs, flat butts, skinny arms, and faces that sag from exertion. (Some say that running can increase the production of free radicals and cause wrinkles, and I'm afraid they're right.) Looking over the starved, pinched physiques of the great Olympic long-distance runners, you're more inspired to reach for a sandwich than copy their desperate race.

More than anything, running is now a matter of fashion. To be brief about it, in our age everything about running, except for the hard work it entails, has become trendy. And fast on the heels of fashion comes business, and vice versa, giving rise to a curious, mindboggling paradox: these days more people dress like runners than actually run.

At first people wore tracksuits, or joggers, the one item of clothing named after the sport for which it was manufactured, which swiftly whipped up a sportswear frenzy. In Italian we call the tracksuit a *tuta*, from the French *tout-de-même*, "all the same" or "all-in-one," a word that perfectly encapsulates the one-piece created in the 1920s by Futurist painter Ernesto Michahelles, alias Thayah, to whom we also owe the neologism TuTa that served as a model for the jumpsuit. A large T was superimposed onto a rectilinear U with wide trouser legs that formed an A.

The combination of hooded sweatshirt and cotton pants soon became the official uniform of Olympic runners at the medal ceremony. After crossing the finish line in shorts and a tank top, athletes would wrap themselves in comfortable, warm jumpsuits to prevent them from catching cold and standing before the public half-naked, the way boxers wear robes into the ring. Called *survêtement* (literally "overclothes") in French, the tracksuit debuted at the 1924 Paris Olympics and was made of velvet. The first to don one was the English runner Olivier Johnson Schofield, who wore it with a tie. A hundred years later, ties retired, the tracksuit is now the uniform for anyone who wants to relax (and dress like it), whether they're out for a stroll or on the road. Sports are rarely the activity of choice for those in a sweatshirt, jogging pants, and a pair of sneakers.

To go from the Olympic games to the closets of every couchbound Westerner, the final paradox in the history of sportswear, the coup de grace of fashion, when athletic clothes became useless for running, when not counter-productive to it, was yet to come. The road that led most sportswear to be "sporty, but not for playing sports" began in the 1980s, when American music videos featured rappers wearing XXL jumpsuits and basketball sneakers so enormous you couldn't run a yard in them. These were followed up in the 1990s with sexualized versions for female pop stars.

The same happened to sneakers. In the 2000s they wandered off the basketball court and infiltrated every non-sports event imaginable, weddings and funerals included. Initially, running shoes didn't succumb to this trend. They're pretty ugly, after all. Not until Nike furnished them with gel cushioning, shiny colors, and a level of comfort that is as hard to beat as it is expensive to buy. The next time you enter a crowded place, be it a train station waiting room or a museum, have a look around. You'll see that nowadays sophisticated running shoes are most often worn by people who aren't running and probably never will.

Sure, the Greeks may have run naked, or almost, but these sociological volte-faces make me feel as old and out of place as Philippides and his lot. The two things I find most surprising about this aesthetic trend that has turned running into *the* philosophy—lifestyle, really—du jour are the speed with which it occurred and the cunningness with which it has been marketed.

As to the speed at which the unathletic have put on sneakers—in the span of two decades!—all I can say is how baffled I've been by what's happened, how it makes me feel forever behind the curve, slow to catch up. I'm only thirty-five but I can remember a time when a sweatsuit was a uniform strictly reserved for the two hours of gym class a day, the way ski pants are reserved for the mountains or a bathing suit for the beach. I'd never dream of wearing a sweatshirt for reasons not connected to sports. The same was true of sneakers. One pair was plenty for my (scant) athletic needs. I remember as a teenager my mother taking me to one of the first big sporting goods stores for my birthday, one of the many that would soon crop up everywhere and get bigger and bigger. I remember how overwhelmed we were staring at all that equipment and sportswear that we hadn't even imagined existed and which were now all the rage, and feeling that we might be left out. Now, as an adult, it's the opposite. My wardrobe is packed with sweatshirts and workout tops and at least three or four pairs of sneakers. Yet none of this activewear is used for being active. I had to pick up a pair of shoes and comfortable pants made specifically for running. One time, traveling for work, I forgot my running shoes and tried to run in a pair of casual sneakers. I had naively assumed that, being sneakers, they could be put to any use, and I wound up nearly tearing my tendon and dislocating my knee.

As for the ingenuity of advertisers, who have turned running into a lucrative fetish, I doff my cap. What they've pulled off is so diabolical that they deserve their own spot in Dante's hell. For reasons of chronology, Dante couldn't have created a circle for these marketing pirates, otherwise he might have condemned them to an eternity of wanting something that doesn't actually exist.

If all that running requires is a road, and it's the cheapest sport around, why is everyone now happy to shell out money for a sport that costs nothing? We're also, it should be said, willing to pay a lot to not run. Between running shoes worn for walking and sneakers for lounging around, I wonder what we think we're buying when we support this modern aesthetic, why we've opted to keep the comfort of tracksuits and sneakers but skip the hard work that they were made for. Look at us. Cozy on the couch, dressed to go out and play.

I don't know whether we're nurturing a collective illusion by dressing up like Olympic champions or don't want to admit we're not champions and never will be, as if we were all putting on a giant masquerade by transforming the streets of our cities into enormous outdoor gyms, or whether it's a way of forgiving ourselves for being desk-bound by pretending that we *could* play sports, we're still ready and *capable* of doing so, if only we weren't so busy. That's the impression we make when we wander around our cities dressed like joggers and mountain climbers.

I don't know what to say. I don't have any answers. I, too, try to strike a balance between running and resting in these weird times. But I do know that the aesthetic categories of an age speak volumes about the society that produces and shares them.

We venerate the athletic body but don't take up the hard work that playing sports demands. Running apparel is most sought after by people who don't want to run. The growth rate of the running industry is in the double digits, as is the growth rate of children and adults living with obesity. We've never run so much, yet we are increasingly overweight and inactive. We run ourselves into the ground just to flaunt our muscles and forget to use them to play sports—any sport whatsoever. It's puzzling that people would rather spend years working their abs and glutes to show them off than run or row or kick around a soccer ball or spar with an opponent. Strength training has become an end in itself, a way for people to say they're in shape and meet today's standards of beauty, standards that would have us all young, even when we're old.

I have the general impression that by running in the latest trendy sports clothes, we're more conscious of our bodies, more turned in on ourselves, more self-involved, and indifferent to anything outside our own narrow circle. Sometimes we seem more neurotic and clearly we're more cut off from others, even the guy jogging a few feet in front of us.

* * *

I've nearly written an entire book about running and in a few weeks I'll be taking part in my first—and maybe last—marathon, but I'm still not sure I've fully grasped why running is so popular. One suffers, one toils, one spends time and money with no hope of winning or coming in first or even improving one's looks. So why do we all do it?

Then, one bright afternoon at the end of September I was running alone through some fields in Brittany, the grass and I were both wilting, and for the first time I could observe myself from outside my physical body. I realized that all this running and training and following workout programs and chasing after purely personal goals had transformed me into the spitting image of solitude, and vanity.

If it's true you run alone even when you run with someone else, I think that there is no one on the face of Earth as voluntarily alone as a runner. I'm not talking about the contemplative, coveted, self-imposed form of solitude that makes running one of the most spiritual sports there is, a private moment of pleasure or pain. I mean a social, almost political solitude that is sought after and paraded around and rejects playing with others.

Had civic isolation a face and a pair of gaping eyes they'd be those carved out by the pained expressions of a runner who places her physical and intellectual energies into an utterly private act like running, who sets individual goals and targets for herself, independent of collective thinking, whose standards of success and failure are suited to her own abilities. One runs as best one can and when one can, but one's triumphs are relative. Also, one doesn't need to study how to run, because we're all naturally capable of placing one foot in front of the other. If running went by any other name, you might accuse it of populism.

What a runner leaves in the dust is the collective aspect of sports, with its rules of play that determine who wins and who loses. She is the one who decides how hard to exert herself. Indeed, her satisfaction depends on her alone, since she establishes the finish line. That's why the outcome of a marathon is relative. It corresponds not to external, objective rankings but to internal, invisible goals that can't be shared with others.

When I run in Athens I won't be running with or against the other participants, but with and against myself. My winning or losing won't mean anything to anyone but me. Everyone has to run the same 26.2 miles, yet all ten thousand long-distance runners that I'll be running alongside in November will be running a different marathon and will have their hearts set on different and highly personal times, goals, and results. It's as if eleven soccer players each had his own idea about when he could claim to have won, and the ref was in on it.

I used to believe that the thousands of us who storm the streets of our cities every day form a kind of large tribe, bound by a set of unwritten rules and united in our suffering. But I was dead wrong. We're hermits. In non-professional running everything is relative—to oneself. There is no more solitary and self-involved sport in the world.

I think this must be one of the many insidious consequences of being immersed in a "performance society."

If achieving a common, objective, selfless goal is considered too onerous after the major movements of the 1960s and '70s, or the shiny patina of wellbeing makes such a goal seem vain, then human beings, who by their nature must yearn for something if they mean to survive, have moved the goalposts. What they deem worthy of their efforts has gone from external to internal, from collective to individual.

From Plato's *Symposium* on, man has been a creature of desire. So long as humans are mortal, they can never be so happy as to stop wanting more. Since our great collective ideals have come crashing down, from government to religion and all the structures of civic engagement in between, happiness has now become so private—and sold pre-privatized at a dear price—we may as well try to manufacture it ourselves and be our own judges and tyrants. Hence the obligation to be permanently performing, to compete every damn morning, so that in the evening we can say we've won (whether we've bested ourselves, our schedules, the gaze of others, or the watch on our wrists doesn't matter). As long as we can taste that crumb of satisfaction that reminds us that we're alive, that gives us permission to pat ourselves on the back and say, "Bravo!"

Up until thirty years ago we took to the streets to stand up for our ideals and demand a more dignified future. Today, we take to the same streets to run alone and in silence, hoping that our individual liberties are earned with six-packs, calves of steel, and a forgettable personal best. *What's your time?* is the first question you're asked when you say you've run a marathon, the height of relativizing the outcome of a race. Occasionally I think that if all the runners clogging the sidewalks of Europe were to take to the streets not to run but to ignite a revolution, no institution of power would be safe. Obviously, my ambitions to change the world are quickly forgotten as I put on my running shoes.

This is how jogging, an activity whose only point is to stretch your legs and feel healthy, has recently developed into running, i.e., an activity with goals, workout routines, recorded times, and iron wills. Running has quickly deteriorated from a lighthearted hobby to a self-imposed pressure cooker, where performance is the watchword, one that best encapsulates our anxiety-inducing times. It has strayed from sports into the field of personal development where one must prove to others, or to oneself, one's worth and one's right to exist.

Amateurs who would practically kill to shave a few seconds off their running time, apparel for surviving extreme weather conditions, outrageous nighttime workouts with headlamps, vitamin supplements of all shapes and sizes, physical therapists, mindfulness coaches . . . There's honor in taking something seriously, but the pressure that many runners put on themselves reveals there's a lot more going on than simply needing to work out and feel fit. In the long run, this kind of oppression that forces us to keep doing better, that demands we run a yard more today than we ran yesterday and a yard less than we will run tomorrow, that we must go a little faster and a little longer before we can claim to be fulfilled, will transform running, and life in general, into a permanent form of autocorrect rather than into a celebration of ourselves.

Homo faber fortunae suae. Man is the maker of his own destiny. The Latin phrase became the maxim of humanism. And it applies to running. What you gain from running is contingent upon how hard you're willing to train. It's fair and honest and can't be avoided. As long as what you're chasing after, during a marathon or on a relaxing morning run, is a good mood and not some unachievable ideal.

Even if you were to run to the ends of the earth there would always be another horizon, a ceiling that cannot be shattered, only lived under and enjoyed. As Philostratus says somewhere in *On Gymnastics,* the same slope can be run up and run down. It depends on who's doing the running.

T he starter pistol won't go off in Greece for another four days, but my marathon began today—at the Louvre.

During my moment of downtime (which precedes every battle), unable to train lest I tire out my muscles before my final challenge, I thought it only natural to let my thoughts run free in a museum. I always come to the Louvre when I need to restore Greece to a solid state, when I want to give back to the idea of the classics, which, while I'm writing, is confined to a nebulous spirit, a body of stone and bronze statuary, of terracotta vases.

I want to stop dwelling on life and running and let myself feel what stuff Greece is made of. I want to linger over a statue so long that I can see exactly where the hammer fell and discern the bristles of the brush that turned an amphora red, or black, 2,500 years ago. That is my idea of resting up before I hop a flight to Athens.

I have no aim in mind. I don't know what I'm looking for. But I am confident that whatever it is, here is where I'll find it, on this Sunday afternoon in the Galeries des Antiques.

Not that I'm holding out hope I'll come across a statue of an ancient runner. I've never seen one here before. Once again, today I stand in front of a glass display with sculptures found around the stadium in Olympus and can admire a whole series of glorious discus throwers, wrestlers, and javelin throwers. But there's no trace of a runner.

Next to Venus de Milo I can't help but notice her chiseled abs. I hadn't been aware of them before. To say nothing of the naked men, masterpieces of artistic anatomy. That splendor of athleticism was destined for a short life, or so it seems as I wander into the hall of Roman antiquities. Though still of unparalleled beauty, these statues gradually go slack, their muscles become less defined, due, perhaps, to an unspoken rule that says anything precious must arrive in slightly diminished form on its journey from Greece to Rome, as if it had been chipped away at, more rough-hewn to suit our Roman tastes, which apparently can't reach the heights of Greek elegance.

After an hour or so—I don't check my watch but I can see out the window that the sunlight on the great pyramid of the Louvre is fading—what I'm left with after all this Greek flesh is an impression of warm sensuality—to the point of having to remove the scarf and coat that I kept on just to avoid leaving them at the coat check. All these bodies—these firm legs, sturdy calves, literally marble backsides, large hands, six-pack abs, and beefy biceps—I feel as if they're begging me to touch them, to caress them. Or maybe it's just me who has this scandalous desire. Staring at a bust of Aphrodite, I'm almost tempted to kiss her on the lips.

My erotic crisis a few days before my marathon must be a side effect of too much running. But it isn't sex that I'm thinking about in front of the statues at the Louvre, but pure and palpable sensuality, so real and magnetic that it almost *demands to be matched with an equally intense will to live. At the feet of these strong Greek bodies immortalized in marble and bronze, I feel dizzyingly mortal this afternoon, even if I'm the one with a beating heart. I'd like to touch them and take with me a little of that glory that makes them imperishable Olympic athletes, hoping to transform into an athlete myself, even for just a couple hours on the plain of Marathon.*

Having gotten over my fit of passion, which nearly landed me in prison instead of Athens, I end my afternoon at the Louvre with what for me has always been and will always be the most beautiful statue in the world: the Nike of Samothrace. Next to, not in front of her. Side-stepping tourists snapping selfies, I stand to the right of Winged Victory to admire the twist of her three-quarter bust and can almost feel the strong Aegean winds beating along the barren Thracian coasts.

For the first time I realize that this woman's wings, poised to take flight, so graceful her feathers appear to flutter, are secured to the body of the statue by a kind of invisible harness. It moves me to think of the proud fragility of that goddess, for whom defeat doesn't exist. I'm put in mind of the one word that Philippides *spoke after running 26.2 miles for the first time in history:* nenikékamen. *The verb comes from* Nike, *but the runner uses the plural form. He isn't celebrating an individual exploit. It isn't one person's boast. It's a victory, the salvation of an entire people—the Athenians.*

Who knows what will happen at my marathon, a race that's run entirely in the first person. I won't risk making predictions or setting goals for myself. I trained as best I could and for once I have no reason to beat myself up. All I want is to arrive at the end of that route and put it behind me.

Maybe that's why my afternoon at the Louvre has ended in front of the Nike of Samothrace. Tired after months of training, my legs have led me to the foot of this statue so that I can naively start my run on the word victory *and not, like* Philippides, *end on it.*

Or maybe, I think, catching myself seated at the foot of a marble woman whose face we can never know, the real reason I came to the Louvre was to pray.

F or Homer, the Greek sea was wine-colored, *oinops pontos*. For me, that violet-verging-on-purple color is the last furious rays of the sun beating down on the sacred tarmac of Athens International.

As usual I can't bear the disconnect between how far we've flown and how long it takes to get there. In a little over three hours we've gone from Paris to Greece, far less time than it'll take me to run my first marathon tomorrow. Sealed inside the cabin of an anonymous airline, squished between my fellow anonymous travelers, I find it hard to feel that I'm now just a few miles from the starting line of this endeavor of legs and spirit that I've spent months training for. Unlike trains—my preferred form of transportation when not going overseas—airplanes give me no sense of the physical space I'm crossing when I travel, no clues to attest to my having flown to Athens and not, say, Rome or Madrid.

Once I'm inside the terminal, Greece forces me to acknowledge its presence, starting with its alphabet. Billboards, placards, signs: every word is set down in those ancient letters that I learned to master as a girl—or maybe *they* mastered me—and once more reassure me. So Attica does exist, it's not all in my head. Not only does it exist, but in a few hours I'll cross it east to west with the strength of my legs alone, if they'll be so kind as to hold out to the end.

I'm not alone. With me is my boyfriend, who has come to Athens to be my motivator and, more importantly, my support system. Waiting for us outside the airport is Nick—a shortened Anglicization of Nikos, I imagine—the owner of the one-bedroom that I've rented in Marathon, since finding a hotel for the night before my race proved impossible. Maybe hotels are closed for the winter. Or maybe no hotels have been opened from the age of Philippides to the present. (I don't know where the other long-distance runners sleep; maybe they stay in Athens and travel these blessed 26.2 miles by car and then by foot, a roundtrip in reverse for the sake of a race.)

After the ordeal of picking out Nick, a large Greek guy in the parking lot wearing socks and flipflops in the middle of November, we cram into his red compact and head to Marathon. I'm excited, agitated, nervous. I try to keep things under control and not wear myself out before the race has even begun. In a few minutes Nick turns onto Marathon Avenue, *Leoforos Marathonos*, a road where traffic speeds by, a kind of beltway that connects the vast and indistinguishable suburbs of Athens to the eastern coast of Attica and ends in front of Euboea, passing by a monotonous series of suburban centers before reaching, twenty miles on, the city of Marathon, a name that immediately calls to mind a battle.

My heart skips a beat and suddenly starts pumping faster when I realize where I am, as if I were surprised that everything that I've spent months tirelessly training for and thinking about exists. I can't say where my incredulousness comes from. What was I expecting? That this was all

194 · ANDREA MARCOLONGO

a joke and I would be released from the obligation of running tomorrow? Maybe it's just me. After twenty years, I still struggle to trust Greece and its wisdom, which always seems *too much*—too big for the Greeks to have thought of and too difficult for me to understand.

A few words is all it takes to realize that our Greek guide knows nothing about Greece, nor is he even interested in knowing anything about it. Seeing my surprise when we pass by the archaeological site where tombs of Athenian soldiers who fell against the Persians are kept, Nick brushes it off as "something, you know, old," and no longer relevant.

He doesn't know he's broken my heart again. How often it's been broken on my visits to Greece, when I come to the sad realization that not everyone here is declaiming Homer on the streetcorner, as I had childishly expected, and that compared to Isocrates your average Greek stuck in a traffic jam speaks a language far less lofty and far more explicit. It must be a symptom or another example of what Nikos Dimou calls the "unhappiness of being (contemporary) Greeks," who find it impossible to forget the majesty of classical Greece and impossible to surpass it, and are condemned to perpetual mediocrity, because the height of their civilization was reached 2,500 years ago and can never be repeated.

Only this time, there's something else, something in addition to my childish disappointment: old age, transience, that unhealthy obsession with death that compelled me to start running three years ago and is the reason I'm here in a car with a stranger in the middle of the plain of Marathon.

Meanwhile Nick is happy to talk soccer with my partner (a more riveting subject of conversation than Philippides' sacrifice, I'm afraid), as we drive along Marathon Avenue one November night, and out my window we pass ugly, empty, rundown warehouses, neon supermarkets and fast-food restaurants, car dealerships and tile companies, and I worry about how long *kleos* lasts.

The Greeks made no promises that *kleos* was permanent or incorruptible. Sure, the ancient hero sought fame and glory with honor and unwavering devotion, even risked his life for it. This word, which can pluck one out of obscurity, is why Hector goes out to face Achilles in the end, why Penelope faithfully waits for Ulysses.

The Greek word for fame, *kleos*, comes from the verb *kluo*, to listen, and literally means "what others hear speak of you." Tonight, surrounded by kebab stands and DIY warehouses, I feel like I'm the one person in Greece who remembers the sacrifice of the first long-distance runner and the many Greek soldiers who preferred to fall at the hands of their enemy rather than cede that side of civilization known as the birthplace of democracy.

But maybe this fame that the Greeks believed one needed in order to dignify his or her existence had an expiration date that eluded me, a deadline after which not even the greatest glory could survive intact in the memory of a people, an awful day when no one "hears speak" of you, good or bad. If that were true, then even the most noble and regal gesture would be vain, destined to fade fast from collective memory—if it ever managed to penetrate it—and clearly from individual memory. And we'd have nothing but sadness to leave to posterity.

If Philippides failed to achieve immortality after running twenty-five miles—he did drop dead upon arrival, after all—how could I have thought for a second that I'd achieve it? That's what I'm thinking, lost in my reveries, as our car finally approaches the outskirts of Marathon. There is nothing peculiar or mythological about the village, now engulfed in darkness. With its cubelike concrete houses, not one of them painted that optic white that graces every postcard of Greece, Marathon could be any small modern-day town cobbled together to attract tourists with recklessly—and illegally—built houses just a step away from the Greek sea.

At the intersection I notice a tobacco shop and next to it a blue sign informing pedestrians—who've stayed home tonight, evidently—at eight o'clock there's no one about, and Marathon seems to be the one city in Europe where no one jogs—that they are treading kilometer four of the first marathon in the history of humankind. Hoping, perhaps, it would be a deterrent, the owner has placed a life-size statue of a Greek warrior next to the vending machine selling cigarettes and other junk. But judging by the cheap plastic of his ridiculous muscles, the statue was probably made in China.

Finally, looking at this facsimile of Philippides actively guarding a rusty shutter, I smile for the first time since we've arrived in Greece. Maybe it doesn't have the whiff of books and is a less spectacular sight than I'd been expecting, but it proves *kleos*, immortal glory, doesn't fade. Here in Greece its feet are firmly planted on the ground.

It's the night air that finally stops my head from spinning and allays my dread, the kind that comes over you the night before a big test—or before your first marathon. It smells of the sea and ancient history, this Greek wind blowing steadily from the Euboean Gulf. It smells of good, solid things, of things that are finally where they should be and will remain there, secure, suited to the edge of time and of lives that pass and die and yet somehow, somewhere remain.

This is where they'll remain forever, at least for me, on this twenty-six-mile-long stretch of land between Marathon and Athens.

* * *

The stone marker on the sidewalk indicating the starting line of the Athens Marathon—which the organizers proudly advertise as the "authentic" marathon, as if races that hadn't been around since ancient times were somehow illegitimate—is patently false. It has no historical value. It's just a convention, like the Greenwich meridian, a reference point for imposing our logic on the world. There is nothing in Herodotus or Plutarch that says this inch of soil is the exact point where Philippides sped off on his two legs and didn't stop until he collapsed at the Panathenaic Stadium.

But today, standing next to this crooked stone cast like dice on the Attic Peninsula, I'm the conventional one who has come here to run her first marathon.

They say that the hardest moment of a marathon aside from the famous "wall" runners hit around mile twenty—which I'm not worried about just now, I haven't even gotten to mile one—occurs before the start of the race, strangely enough. Whether it's a few minutes or a day or a week before the pistol shot, there comes a time when every long-distance runner—neophytes especially, though not even experienced runners are impervious to changes of heart—looks at the road ahead with watery eyes and wonders, "Who the hell put me up to this?"

For me this un-Socratic doubt crept in that evening before going to bed, while I was laying out my running clothes for the next day with painstaking care on the kitchen table (Nick the Greek's table): industry standard, big-brand black leggings; candy pink gym socks, a little nod to the marathon's having made me both aware of my feminine side and proud of it; a black off-brand running jacket that I'd worn to tatters—the zipper on its left pocket was broken—and is particularly dear to me, a good luck charm, the first jacket I bought when I caught running fever. It has kept me warm during all those workout sessions when I'm sure I'll never make it. It wouldn't be until after I'd left the house that I discovered in its broken pocket a note of encouragement and love—which are one and the same thing—from my partner.

In a two-bedroom apartment in the middle of the Attic Peninsula, I lay in the dark for several minutes, or hours, bitterly asking myself why, at the end of the day, I was willing to put myself through this, why I was so determined to run a marathon. I'm the one who wanted this, I brought this on myself, and to reach my goal I've dedicated a frankly outrageous amount of time and energy, not to mention all the pages of a book whose beating heart is running itself.

Last night, as the wind beat against the house and seemed to moan through Marathon, the hard and inescapable slog awaiting me at the starting line of the most historic marathon in the world appeared to be, for me personally, what it always was. Pointless. Superficial. How pointless and superficial of me to try to prove to myself and others—but mostly myself, I imagine—that thanks to a pair of sturdyish ankles, a heart rate that happens to have won the genetic lottery, and two lungs that by some miracle have survived all the smoking and sitting around, I am capable, I am strong and talented, I deserve to be admired and honored or at least have someone patiently waiting at the finish line say "Way to go!" all because one fine day I decided to go out for a run.

But what I most hope to prove by this pathetic effort is that I still have time, that adulthood (read: old age) is relative, as obscenely terrified people such as myself like to say. That if I was able to impose on my life such a punishment that it enabled me to run a marathon from start to finish, then that meant that nothing is definitive and there is no end to youth if you dedicate yourself to staying in shape. That no choice is irreversible. That no time is wasted. And the next morning I can get back to reinventing myself, to rewriting once again the character I am in my story, just as I've done by my surprise turn as a runner.

Oh, shut up, I thought tonight. Besides all of my half-baked, Freudian speculations, the fact that I am physically and financially able to wake up on a November morning in the heart of Greece and run 26.2 miles (or "just" the original twenty-five miles) is incontrovertible proof that I live and prosper in a part of the world that is blessed with useless problems and pointless labors, and the clearest and most outrageous example of that is the marathon I'm about to run.

Finally, dawn, no bigger than a stamp, does me the courtesy of entering my window and stands beside the bed where, like a lover, I've spent all night pleading for him to show up. On the day of my first marathon, dawn really is *rododaktulos*, rosy-fingered, as Homer has it. Putting on my running shoes, I only now realize that the phrase is neither romantic nor sacred. Instead, it perfectly captures the lofty skies of Greece, sun-streaked like the coat of a panther.

I snap a photo of the sunrise and send it to my editor, who supported my bizarre venture and is waiting in Rome for news of my race, if for no other reason than to be assured I'll bring it to a conclusion and then, my legs once more tucked under a desk, hurry up and finish this book. A few other things—a kiss for my sleeping partner who'll be waiting for me in Athens later, as strong a reason as epic *kleos* to totter all the way to the entrance of Panathenaic Stadium—and I'm ready to go. Or so I think and hope.

I open the door and push aside the mosquito net required by law in Greece—useless in November but ever present. The plain of Marathon spread out before me is dotted with reeds blowing gently in the wind. On the horizon, to the west, I glimpse mountains no bigger than hills. To the east the immortal Greek sea that will continue to flow south all the way to Piraeus.

For a moment I recall Philostratus writing in *On Gymnastics* about conviction and coaches ready to stake their lives on their athletes. (About athletes seized with fear and panic before a race, he remains silent.) I don't have coaches and cheerleaders ready to die for me, fortunately. And yet, it occurs to me now as I walk nervously toward the starting line of my race on this solemn morning, I do have a book.

A book isn't a life, I know, but almost. Or maybe it's more than that. In any case, it's the one good reason I can find this morning to wipe off the cold sweat of anxiety and futility, and I take my place next to that stone stuck in the red earth of Marathon with the distance to Athens scored brazenly across it: twenty-five miles.

* * *

First six miles under my belt and I feel great. I literally feel like an ancient goddess of running who has made a grand entrance this morning after standing for centuries on the side of the road between Marathon and Athens.

I pop off my heels with genuine happiness, almost laughing, and synchronize my stride with my heartbeat. The winter sun strikes my face, which I keep aimed at my goal, as if I were drinking up the Greek light. I'm exhilarated, overjoyed really, as if running this marathon were the most beautiful thing I'd done in my life. I drink it all in, unslakable: the rhythm of my feet on the pavement, the semi-divine lightness with which they touch down and gently rise off the ground a moment later.

I have always loved running once past the three-mile threshold—or rather, ever since I was able to run them without suffocating. I still find the start of a run to be wearisome, unnatural, even ridiculous as I stupidly struggle to defy gravity and all the laws of aerodynamics that make the erect human body cumbersome and unfit for the animal elegance of running. There have been many days when at mile one or two I have nearly burst into tears, this close to turning home and never going out for a run again. It's always at the start—of a workout, a romantic relationship, a book to write—that my mind does nothing but scream like a siren, "You'll never make it!" And yet I always make it.

My whole body—legs, heart, lungs—are holding up rather well, chugging along comfortably. Despite the panicked shouts in my head, my organs aren't about to poop out, surprisingly. If I succeed in distracting myself by doing anything besides stopping, and if I dare to believe in my body, and like Ulysses escape the cruel sirens of running unscathed, well then, after a few, painful warm-up miles, which at the end of the day are manageable, I find myself so pleasantly caught up in the footrace that I could sing along with the Boss: "Born to run—that's me!"

While I pass by signs indicating how far we've come from Marathon—five kilometers, seven, thirteen, sixteen—I feel so good, so energized, so self-possessed, master of my body and mind, that I seriously begin to think that the gods—or a god—are smiling down on me, at least on Greek turf. Or maybe it's karma. Maybe what has been reawakened is a memory of the countless lives that have crossed this plain before me, bent on winning athletic and poetic competitions.

Everything around me seems beautiful, though thinking about it now, as I write and sift through my mental notes from that day, it could hardly be called beautiful.

I'm not sure I've seen the "fennel" from which the word *marathon* is derived, but after almost two hours I seem to have catalogued all the vegetables that will be plucked from these Greek fields and in a few days stock the shelves of European supermarkets. I'm surrounded by a giant vegetable garden with perfectly neat rows that turn the entire field of Marathon into a green checkered tablecloth spread over the slopes of Athens. It's not the dramatic blue sky over Greece that overpowers me as I run today but the utterly green fields all around me, so that I forget the presence of the sea, hidden away, a few miles to the east.

One of the motivating factors behind my steady clip and firmness of purpose are the stray dogs that mill about the sidewalks and street corners. Staring into their hollow, unpitying yet dignified eyes, I find myself thinking about breeding, about the handful of chromosomes and genetic accidents that ultimately make us what we are. Who knows how much crossbreeding and mongrelizing went on to produce these Greek dogs that look at me like I'm mad—and for good reason! Who knows what heroic canines they descend from. Who knows if three thousand years ago one of their ancestors met Argos, Ulysses' loyal companion.

The sight of a shepherd patiently leading his goats along the banks of a creek fills me with such bucolic delight that I feel like the protagonist of one of Theocritus's idylls and forget about the wind blowing a little too fiercely on my face, which is now purple from the cold and fatigue. This uncontrollable, crazy joy, which will soon come to an end, reaches its peak when I put out my hand, snatch a bitter olive from a tree on the side of the road, and pop it in my mouth, a snack of sorts. Protein bars and running gels can't, I tell myself, top the millennial energy stored inside the roots of a Greek olive tree, Athena's sacred gift.

* * *

As I think back on it now, it was clear that I was suffering from an attack of hubris or some chemical reaction produced in my oxygen-deprived brain that, lacking all else, filled me with a euphoric high. This bitter realization came to me around the ten-mile mark, as the beautiful green fields and tidy gardens of Marathon gave way to bathroom supply warehouses and snarling traffic, just as Murakami describes in his book. (Like me, Murakami chose this sacred traditional route for his first solo marathon, except he ran in the opposite direction, from Athens to Marathon.)

Then my happiness came to a screeching halt, like chalk scraping a blackboard. And I began to sense the cold, to feel tired, hungry, achy.

Suddenly Athens seemed far away, and I had never felt so alone.

* * *

The salty scent of the sea mixes with the smell of kerosene heaters kicking in on a winter morning. I'm not so sure I'll make it.

It isn't that some part of me is in pain, exactly. True, my legs are beginning to stiffen from the exertion and my left ankle is a bit inflamed, but all in all my body isn't showing any signs of giving up. No, my legs keep going forward. It's my mind that is sowing the seeds of doubt.

I don't know who's doing the talking, my consciousness, my unconscious fears, the cells that make up my muscles, which are now running low on glycogen, or the infuriated ghost of Philippides. Just a whisper at first, then a buzzing, then a shrill voice becomes distinct, and finally nagging, nonstop chatter. Suddenly, as I'm nearing eighteen miles, the military tribunal sitting in judgement over my half-hearted long-distance runner's soul starts to express serious doubts about my ability to see this competition through.

"Will I make it?" I start to wonder, increasingly worried.

"How much farther?" I keep checking the miles left until the finish line but to no avail. The idea that I just need to repeat the titanic effort that got me this far is cold comfort. It literally brings tears to my eyes, making me feel like a stupid masochist.

Gone the idiotic smile of a couple miles back, as I brazenly crossed the plain of Attica believing I was the offspring of Atalanta. In its place a crooked scowl has crusted over my face. I struggle to keep my eyes open as a biting wind seems bent on driving me back whence I came, rather than propelling me to Athens. Now I know why it took Ulysses so long to get back to Ithaca. My chin and cheeks are so red and chapped I have the impression they might slide right off my face. My hands I keep clenched and out in front, prepared to punch an invisible enemy who has the nerve to cut me off. In my ears I hear the tragic chorus of my friends who, hearing news of my crazy endeavor, keep asking, "Why are you punishing yourself?"

The 92 metopes of the Parthenon—which, if I survive, I hope to visit with my partner tomorrow—depict scenes of violence and anguish inspired by the first battle between order and chaos, between animal instinct and rational thought. Led by Phidias, skilled Athenian sculptors carved Centaurs, Amazons, Lapiths, and Giants in their final senseless assault on Olympus. Half-naked and animal-like, drunk and enraged, these forsaken creatures have sat atop the Acropolis for centuries, caught in the definitive, immortal moment that would forever turn them into myth and cosmogony: the moment of their fall.

That's more or less how I feel now, like a fallen Giant or

wounded Amazon, as I round the eighteen-mile mark and run straight into the black hole of my marathon. The Wall.

The Wall is as easy to grasp as it is hard to describe, yet the name perfectly conveys the sense of coming crashing down. All of a sudden your body declares its reserves of energy have been exhausted: you haven't a drop left, and every single cell seems to scream before collapsing. One by one, the muscles you built during your workouts, which had thus far held up, go limp, as if the god of running in the engine room of this hopeless marathon were sadistically switching off all the levers that enable your fibers and tendons to function smoothly.

I feel bled dry, as if the race had drained what the Greeks call *pneuma*, the life force underneath my skin, which is right now being harassed by the Greek wind. My pointless efforts seem to have worn down both my muscles and the soles of my shoes, and all that's left of me is this outer covering, like the skin of the lion hunted by Hercules, and its desire to plop down on the corner of Marathon Avenue and wait for someone to gather her up quickly, like wastepaper, is almost touching.

The Wall, as it refers to the physical and moral exhaustion that comes over almost every athlete before the end of a marathon (if they haven't already collapsed), is exclusive to running. No other sport, however demanding, comes close to the grueling aerobic workout that is long-distance running, which literally consumes the carbs stored in your liver and muscles. Like a car that has run out of gas or a cell phone with no battery, the body has given all it's got to reach this point of the race. If out of sadism, stubbornness, or ambition you really want to keep running until you've arrived at twenty-five miles, then you'll have to seek out that energy somewhere else.

Given the present wooziness of my muscles, I am completely taken aback when, a few hundred yards on, my legs are still plowing ahead. They haven't come tumbling down. I don't know exactly what is propelling them toward Athens or preventing them from falling apart. Apparently, when you think you have nothing left in you, you still have a little more to give. This is where motivation—which I was afraid my anxiety and despondency last night in Marathon had robbed me of—takes the place of depleted muscles and frayed nerves. I have no intention of giving up, not now. I must finish this race, even if it takes days, and I insist on going to see the Giants and Lapiths atop the Parthenon with my own two eyes, standing on my own two legs.

I take in my surroundings, the Mediterranean banlieue that is the outskirts of Athens: Turkish bakeries, rusty scooters, Asian import/export companies, buildings so kitsch I can't tell if they're houses or tombs, and I begin cataloging everything that catches my eye in order to shut out the despotic voice that keeps repeating, "You'll never make it!"

I'll make it, you'll see. Or so I tell myself, meanwhile planning everything, with an almost paranoid level of detail, that I intend to do once this hell is over. What enables Murakami to complete this run is the mirage of an ice-cold beer. For me, it's the dream of a glass—a bottle, rather—of retsina, the popular Greek wine fermented with resin since ancient times. And the Aleppo pines that give retsina its flavor, a blend of the sea and forest, grow right here in Attica.

I can already picture myself at a tavern in Monastiraki listening to someone play ancient heroic music and determined to get drunk and laugh with gusto at these Greeks.

Not satisfied with haunting me my whole life with the bulk and seductiveness of their literature and *philosophie fatale*, now they've sentenced me to run like a madwoman for over twenty-five miles. With the warm sweat beading my forehead turning cold at the touch of the wind, then evaporating, at around mile twenty I swear again and again that I never want to hear another word about them and their foreign tongue, their ancient ideas, their backbreaking sports.

As I'm cursing the Greeks and everything that up until this pathetic moment I've spent my whole life believing in, by some miracle I forget the pain, the fatigue, the dejection. And to my surprise I find myself on the other side of the wall.

* * *

Athens has never looked so ugly as it does a few miles from Panathenaic Stadium. Which is to say, so beautiful.

I have an acute sense of the ground beneath my feet and the rise and fall of my shoes on the crumbling Athens concrete. The rhythm of my steps has become a sort of silent mantra, the heartbeat of this marathon reminding me that, against all odds, I'm just a mile from the finish and still running.

The closer I get to the end of this race, the more I feel the history of Greece underfoot. All the miles I've run from Marathon to Athens have wrought a kind of temporary miracle: for a few hours I'm no longer the puny person being carried on the shoulders of giants. This race has granted me the privilege of walking the never-ending road of human thought on my own two legs, pressing my small feet into the footsteps of those who came before me.

Philippides, on the other hand, appears to have been totally absent. He never even crossed my mind. I didn't see him proudly striding next to me, the very first of his kind, a make-believe running partner; his immortal glory didn't illuminate my passage through Athens. Not for a second.

Surely I'm just exhausted, dehydrated, in desperate need of sugars and rest, yet I suddenly seem to grasp all those things that eluded me when I was awkwardly standing still.

I had to run twenty-five miles to find out how conceited and naïve it is to think that one can circumvent pain. Like the hunted, we run harder when we're wounded.

Having put my body through the wringer, I understood that if I was still running, it was only thanks to the pain, that I was moving my legs *in* pain, that suffering was my companion and cheerleader, not my enemy. On the contrary, running a marathon without agony would be an absurd waste of time. In running and in life, pain is a respectable trophy, win or lose. It's the concrete proof that we're still alive, that if it hurts that is because life is still playing with us, so we might as well play along—that we only fear death when we love life too much. That is the one reason every runner carries on as if she were one of the damned.

I understood that if I can run for hours across the ancient, barren plain of Marathon without getting bored this morning, then nothing in this life will ever bore me. I understood that my mind, which for years I wrestled with before running finally brought me a little peace, is not a minefield to recoil from. It's a shelter, a refuge, where I may not always be comfortable but at least I can take shelter when the debris of the outside world rains down on me.

This is what running this marathon has meant for me,

in a nutshell: not spontaneous joy or pure psychophysical pleasure. The moment of magical ecstasy hasn't arrived and I don't think it ever will. But pain? I've had plenty of that. Still, there was also the feeling of being protected, of being shielded for a few hours from the slings and arrows that overwhelm me whenever I stop moving.

I also understood that there are sublime moments that cannot be rationalized, only felt—and should be fiercely believed in. That there are convictions to pursue with an unshakeable faith closer to religion than statistical probability, that if you believe in something enough, whatever that might be, then it will happen. And if it doesn't happen, that's because you weren't able to believe in it with your whole being.

At last I understood that, by some strange twist of fate or mysterious and perfect alignment of the stars, Greece torments me when I'm not in Greece. When I'm away from its nervous sea and its red earth I chase after it like a fanatic, with no hope of understanding its language, its philosophy, its literature. But when I'm here, a few feet from the Acropolis, it all seems perfectly clear, even if I lack the words to describe it. Everything proves coherent, orderly, destined to last an eternity.

Finally, I realized that no matter how much breath I expend recounting what I have felt while running this marathon, I'll never be able to communicate it to others, or even, in part, to myself. I ran—a lot—but little of what I felt can be translated into words and reason. A large portion of this race will be kept locked inside my burning muscles and tendons and this body hardwired for one thing only: for living.

I'm almost surprised when I suddenly spot the shell of Panathenaic Stadium standing in a cup in the hills covered with pine trees, between Mets and Pangrati. For the past seven miles or so I had stopped thinking of the race as a torture to escape as soon as possible, and now I'm almost sorry that it's coming to an end.

Impressive—or imperious?—it knocks me off balance. For the first time since leaving Marathon this morning I feel the tears coming and badly want to cry. Suddenly I feel surrounded not only by Philippides but by all the Greek athletes that were crowned victors here at the Panathenaic games of Athens.

I spot my partner in the crowd. Just the sight of him moves and comforts me. I try saying something to him but my thoughts seem to come from far away. Being stuck in my head, focused on the race for over four hours, has so shielded me from the outside world that I'm like a fish removed from its tank or a butterfly its cocoon, a new marathoner forced out of the warm womb of running.

After a few minutes of being trapped in my head I realize that twenty-five miles on I've arrived in Athens, the heart of the running world. This is the endpoint, from here on out it's celebration, rest, my post-first-marathon life.

Unlike Philippides I haven't died at the foot of Panathenaic Stadium. True, I'm exhausted, sweaty, chafed, weary, and hungry, but now I can exercise a right that twenty-five miles ago I couldn't. I can join the chorus of runners who, since the Battle of Marathon in 490 BC to today, have had the pleasure and honor of saying nenikékamen.

We've won!

X
RECOVERING

What makes me happy right now is knowing that I
don't have to run another step. Whew!—I don't have
to run anymore.

—HARUKI MURAKAMI

I t's been three weeks since my first marathon and I've
almost forgotten my run.

I write *almost* because, twenty days on, my legs still
ache from my reckless endeavor. In the morning, when I
begrudgingly slip out of bed, some part of me creaks in the
early winter cold, I don't know whether it's my bones or
tendons that are stiff and chilled after all the wind I took on
the plain separating Marathon and Athens.

As for the rest, no one seems to have the faintest memory
of the toll it took to run those miserable twenty-five miles.
Not even me. Sometimes I suspect I never ran them at all.
So powerful is my impression that it was all a pointless
dream that were someone to tell me it was just a projection
brought on by months of writing a book about running I
would accept it unquestioningly.

Exhibit A of my oblivion: the other night my French
editor called. I was in a hurry. When he asked me about my
trip to Greece, I answered distractedly, "What marathon?"

A blister on my big left toe, nearly healed. After three
weeks, that's the one thing I have left to show for all my
running grit.

Everything else—the satisfaction, the valor, the sense

of transcending my personal limitations, the pride and glory—has vanished without a trace. I have the impression that that palpable feeling of accomplishment never even came to pass.

Not that I was expecting pomp and circumstance at the end of the marathon. Well, maybe a little. I would have appreciated a convivial, ancient Olympic style symposium held in my honor, replete with poems to immortalize my victory. My partner saw to that; as soon as I entered the stadium he crowned me with a laurel wreath that he had bought from one of the many savvy street vendors who post up at the entrance.

I knew that for me completing the run from Marathon to Athens wasn't going to change my life or draw a line between a before and after. I didn't believe then and don't believe now that running an entire marathon is an existential matter. At best it's an excellent source of stories to impress a lazy or distracted audience. Still, I had expected that this story of Philippides and epic runs in Attica would have left a mark, inside and out, which, however fleeting, would have lasted a few days, rather than evaporating faster than the sweat that had bathed my forehead for over four hours.

It's almost touching to think that I only recently grasped the imbalance between my inner feelings and outer reality. It is another lesson, the last lesson, the parting gift of this marathon. To acknowledge it came as a shock. I found the disparity violent and barbaric yet real, evident. However important this marathon was to me—however many months I lived with the idea of running it, training for it, imagining it—I forced and encouraged myself to—it had no outward effect.

It seemed natural that the whole world should feel by osmosis the power and urgency of running that I felt. But the world didn't feel a thing. I was what Virginia Woolf in *A Writer's Diary* calls "merely a sensibility."

In short, I will always remember two things about this grueling adventure of legs and spirit: how much pain had to be endured and for how long. And how little time, almost no time at all, it took to forget it.

* * *

People say losing is hard, and far be it from me to disagree. I wish I didn't know, actually. But I do. I can confirm just how much, just how badly, defeat stings. Whether in life or at a game doesn't matter.

But winning seems overrated—if you can (for purely practical reasons) call my having reached the finish line alive winning.

What I mean is, were I to be asked how long the pain lasted after a fall, and how long the memory of pain lasted after the injury scarred over, I'd say months and years and not bat an eye. In some cases, the pain never went away.

Whereas my delight at having completed the first marathon in my life seemed to last little more than five minutes. It didn't even possess the intensity to morph into happiness, that form of beatitude that floods and supports every other aspect of existence, multiplying ideas and energies. Instead it remained a wispy trace of joy, which gave way to an average good mood, a bright halo that disappeared in a jiff.

I seem to recall Andre Agassi saying as much in his memoir *Open* when he makes the outrageous claim that winning his first Wimbledon didn't give him any personal satisfaction, that winning doesn't change a thing. "Now that I've won a slam," he writes, "I know something that very few people one earth are permitted to know. A win doesn't feel as good as a loss feels bad, and the good feeling doesn't last as long as the bad. Not even close."

As soon as I was in the taxi on my way to the apartment, ragged as a stray animal, I had the feeling that the meaning of my physical and mental labors was receding along with the stadium. It was as if the stadium were the epicenter of my reasons for running. And after a good hour under scalding hot water, I noticed that my sense of satisfaction was waning, that other thoughts of various urgency had rushed in to take up space in my head, that I was already worrying about other things, that I didn't have some great epiphany after running twenty-five miles, and in fact I wanted to move on to the next thing as quickly as possible.

The Greeks had a word for treating these feelings of emptiness and stress that come over you after a match: *apoterapia*, or "the moment-after treatment," from *therapeia* (treatment) and *apo* (a preposition meaning from, away from, ending). Once again it is Galen, the original physician, who describes how some trainers in the ancient world would coach athletes before, during, *and* after competitions. Apotherapists, in short.

I've always been unprepared for the moment after, in life and at this marathon. Apparently I've never received apotherapy.

I still remember how down I used to get after a college exam, the mix of extreme tiredness and *horror vacui* I felt, my terror upon discovering what came after a test that for months had been the only date on my calendar. Nothing. Or close to nothing. That's what lay hidden behind a date that I had built up as my be-all and end-all. It was the same now. But maybe it had been true at elementary school, too, when I suffered just as much or more over short quizzes and tests, placing a disproportionate amount of importance on something just to hear my teacher say, "Nice work." The pleasure of getting a good grade, even the best grade, wasn't equal to the effort and dedication it took to attain it.

The joy of passing a test wasn't on par with the days and weeks of anxiety and hard work that I put into passing it. I could never handle being feted. In fact I often avoided sharing news of my successes, large or small, so that I wouldn't have to pretend to be happy. I believe this will also hold true for my long run from Marathon to Athens.

I've never met a single runner who, having arrived at the finish line, sweaty and wiped out after running for miles (anyone who sees footraces as a means to look pretty should take a glance at the monstrous purple faces of runners as they cross the finish line) has an ounce of energy left to celebrate. Some may manage to relax their facial muscles into a smiling grimace, but far more weep with desperation upon clearing the last hundred feet. I, too, felt tears come to my eyes when I glimpsed the Panathenaic Stadium. And it's a fact that everyone shuts their eyes at the exact moment they cross the finish. People not familiar with the profundity of racing are justified in thinking that it is crazy to run twenty-six miles and then, having achieved your goal, refuse to look.

If a runner shuts her eyes at the end, it's because she wants to prolong her race for a moment before being called back to the sluggish rhythms of normal life. What she sees behind her shut eyelids are not celebrations or trophies, but all the workouts, sacrifices, falls, and persistence that it took her to get there, and she is thanking them one by one.

Despite my modest performance, even I felt reluctant about immediately "leaving" the protected, intimate space of *my* run. I know I appeared brusque and unheroic, but I was bothered, almost irked by people who wanted to talk and celebrate my race the second I'd stopped running. What do these people want, I wondered. Why are they forcing me to smile? Why do I have to pretend to be happy just to avoid disappointing them?

Whether you celebrate publicly or privately, as far as running is concerned moment-after therapy involves managing the grief we're accustomed to when things come to an end as well as the painful severance of being physically and emotionally called back to earth and having to tuck your legs under your desk again.

It doesn't matter if you're pleased with yourself or disappointed. The moment after a marathon, you stop joyfully running and revert to walking, marching forward for a lifetime, all the way to the grave.

There's a rule, named after Jack Foster, the New Zealand long-distance runner who came up with it, that calls for one day of rest for every mile raced. Or, if you want to spoil yourself, one day on the couch for every mile of a marathon.

According to Foster's rule, after my race across the Attican Peninsula, I was looking at a minimum of twenty-six days of recovery, forty-two max. Less than three weeks after my first marathon, I defied the rule this morning and, without giving it a second thought, went out for a run.

It was pleasant, more pleasant than I'd expected. And definitely far more pleasant than the exhausting workouts that led me to Athens, when I would swear up and down that, if I ever ran those godforsaken twenty-five miles, I'd never run again in my life.

Even before my marathon, I experienced the same crisis that Murakami describes in his book. I thought that once I'd finished my whacky literary track-and-field project I'd never want to talk about running again. I pictured myself practicing any sport but running, even extreme sports, for the rest of my life. Nobody runs in heaven, I told myself. I equated bliss with hanging up one's running shoes for good.

And yet this morning, under a faint early December sun on the Seine, running seemed so natural, so perfectly wedded to my routine and existence. In my ears a podcast about the spectacular life of Josephine Baker and around me Christmas lights strung up over the streets of Paris, like rainbows.

Nothing hurt. My legs, tendons, lungs, and heart have recovered from the exertion in Attica. Like me, they've forgotten. I had on the same tattered jacket that I wore that day, my sporty version of a Proustian madeleine, concrete proof of my having run that marathon, and a ridiculous neon yellow hat, and gloves and a balaclava to shield against the cold air. I could not have cared less about how long I ran, I just wanted to feel good, to get my feelings—my thoughts—in order, to stretch my legs a little.

For the past few days I'd observed that my "resting

state" wasn't all that restful. I felt irritable, antsy about being so physically immobile and psychologically restless. To sit still and write about the miles I ran to Athens came as a struggle. The sentences trickled onto the page already tired, listless, as if they'd written themselves after a bad night's sleep.

I'm not the only rulebreaker, nor the most brazen. Nearly all runners flout the regulations of post-marathon convalescence and, as soon as they feel sufficiently firm on their feet, lace up their sneakers and get back to pounding the pavement. It's almost impossible to stand still after twenty-five miles. That's why a marathon is rarely an isolated incident on the list of a runner's achievements, a one-off that isn't followed up with other marathons. In my case, the running fever is so far advanced that I've already signed up for San Silvestre Vallecana, the spectacular 10K that lights up the streets of Madrid on December 31.

I'm not sure I'll run another marathon again. My gut says yes, my head says no, the rest of my body says it's too soon to think about. After twenty-five miles my head is the part of me most in need of convalescence, more than my legs. What I am sure of is that running will remain an important part of my life. If not the best at least the most honest. Should I feel like investing the time and energy in the future, I know that my calves will answer the call. Running might not feature prominently in my biography or come naturally, but I do think it will be a mainstay of my life. Or at least something that I finally fully believe in.

So that was it. This morning I decided I'd remain committed to running. I don't intend to turn my back on all that running has taught me nor on the honest part of myself that I discovered through running.

And even if I still happen to walk from one mile to the next, I'd like to think that from here on out the life I lead will keep a running rhythm.

ACKNOWLEDGMENTS

If I've reached the end of this book unscathed, it isn't owing to me but to my fortunate genes which gave me the physical strength to weather a twenty-five-mile run. So thanks to the god or fate responsible. Thanks to my legs, my ankles, my muscles, my tendons, my slow heart rate, my lungs, and every cell in my body. And thanks to the word "running," which apparently is inscribed somewhere in my DNA. Or in my soul.

Thank you to Giovanni Carletti and Ludovic Escande, my Italian and French editors, respectively, for believing in this bizarre project when I didn't and for having continued to believe in it on the *many* occasions I wanted to abandon both running and writing about running.

Thank you to my partner Luis Miguel, who stood by me for the entire writing process, from the time this book was just a foggy idea to the time we sat side by side as I silently proofread the manuscript at a university cafe on Boulevard Saint-Germain. I couldn't have asked for a better motivator, for my calves or my pen, to say nothing of my heart. The real runner in our household is you, my man with the legs of a Greek hero.

Thanks as always to my beloved dog, who every morning, with no apparent gift for sports but a tremendous amount of loyalty, is happy to run by my side along the Seine, oblivious to everything, me especially.

My last and sincerest thanks go to all the runners with whom I crossed paths while writing this book. You may not have known it, but all the (many) times you overtook me and the (rare) times I lapped you, in every sort of weather, you gave me reason not to give up, to trust myself a little, and most importantly to keep running and writing.